Not Room Enough

Not Room Enough

Mexicans, Anglos, and Socio-economic Change in Texas, 1850–1900

Kenneth L. Stewart
Arnoldo De León

University of New Mexico
Press
Albuquerque

Library of Congress Cataloging-in-Publication Data

Stewart, Kenneth L., 1949–
  Not room enough: Mexicans, Anglos, and socio-economic change in Texas, 1850–1900 / Kenneth L. Stewart, Arnoldo De León.
    p.   cm.
  Includes bibliographical references and index.
  ISBN 0-8263-1437-6
  1. Mexican Americans—Texas—Economic conditions.
  2. Mexican Americans—Texas—Social conditions.
  3. Texas—Ethnic relations.
  4. Texas—Economic conditions.
  5. Texas—Social conditions.
I. De León, Arnoldo, 1945–
II. Title.
F395.M5S74   1993
305.8687'20764—dc20   93-13110
                                       CIP

Contents

CONTENTS

Preface

Structural change unprecedented in Texas unfolded during the late nineteenth century. Although Texans of all origins responded to the new opportunities, not all derived equal benefits. This book studies those forces that brought about the structural shifts of the era and explores reasons why new opportunities produced such disparate results. For the subjects of the investigation, change meant gain for Anglos, but degradation for Mexicans.

At least three key historical factors converged to affect developments in the social structure of Texas during the nine-teenth century. First was the successful establishment of Anglo-American rule following the war for independence in 1836. This meant that a new form of government, with specific notions of democracy, supplanted Spanish-Mexican authority.

Immigration also acted to trigger change. The influx of people from the United States, Europe, and Mexico increased in the years after independence, and acceler-ated even more after 1850. The immigrants brought many subtle changes to Texas, but Anglo Americans outnum-bered other groups so that the stability of their political rule went unchallenged. In the end Anglos comprised the host culture and looked upon non-Anglos as foreigners.

The third, and in the authors' view, the key histori-cal force generating structural change, was the shift from frontier conditions toward the modern-day society of twentieth-century Texas. This transformation was essen-tially an economic change, occurring in the latter decades of the nineteenth century. Unfolding unevenly it was most pronounced in central Texas at first, but a drive toward modernity swept the state after the 1870s.

The movement from frontier toward modernity dur-ing the late nineteenth century involved the application of new technology to the means of production and distribu-tion. Sociologically speaking modernization is a process of social change initiated by harnessing inanimate sources of energy and incorporating them into commodity pro-duction and distribution based on machine technology. Once underway the sequence affects economic structures by replacing craft and home-based production proce-dures, restructuring employment opportunities, expand-ing markets and commerce networks, and giving rise to new forms of investment, organization, and control over production and distribution activities. Simultaneously it has implications for social institutions such as politics

and government, household and family patterns, and education. Thus modernization refers to the transformations
in social institutions that occur in conjunction with technologically induced industrialization.

By describing social change in Texas between 1850
and 1900 as a transition from frontier toward modernity,
we do not claim that the social system manifested no
signs of industrialization and modernization before 1850,
nor that the state fully industrialized and modernized by
1900. What we do assert is that the direction of change in
this period was toward industrialization and modernization. After all both industrialization and modernization
refer to more than the social dynamics denoted by the
sociological use of the words. Both processes are historical and unfold in a long-term time frame. The changes we
describe are part of a longer transformation.[1]

There is nothing inherent in the impulses toward
change in late-nineteenth-century Texas to cause inequalities to spring up among people. Thus we begin with
the assumption that the histories of Tejanos (Texans of
Mexican heritage) and Anglo-Texans, though different in
many respects, have essential similarities. To appreciate
this point, it must be remembered that it was Spanish-
Mexicans who first brought the trappings of European
civilization to Texas. It was they who first propagated
Christianity on the Texas frontier. It was they who first
engendered a political structure rooted in principles com-
mensurate with the tenets of European democratic liber-
alism. It was also they who first came to Texas with the
spirit of the frontier; in that spirit they opened the first
acres of range- and farmland to commercial purposes. It
was Tejanos, not Anglos, who first developed policies and
strategies for economic and social progress in Texas.

We do concede that Tejano images of liberal government and progress were at variance with those of
their Anglo-American neighbors. Their language was dif-

ferent, and their ideals descended from a different version of the Enlightenment. They were, for example, more skeptical than Anglos about utilitarian views of social progress, and especially about the possibility of achieving an identity between individual and community interests through a laissez-faire political and economic strategy. They preferred an approach directed at securing the interests of the community and state over and above those of the individual. Nevertheless the essential goals of the nineteenth-century idea of progress, especially those of representative government and capitalist economic development, were as much a part of Tejano as of Anglo dreams about Texas.

In recognition of this essential similarity of interests and aspirations, the analysis that follows treats the central question of why Texas has not been a "land of room enough" for its Hispanic population.[2] We view the history of Texas as a course of events in which two major ethnic groups, Tejanos and Anglos, with similar inclinations toward social progress, competed with one another to realize their goals. Differences in such areas as social status, occupations, poverty, and literacy were consequences of the competition rather than explanations for it. History, in other words, will be presented in this analysis as a force that shapes and molds the differences among people, not one that merely manifests these differences.

A second important goal of this work is to uncover Anglo and Mexican responses to historical and social change. What flexibility and strengths did each display under evolving circumstances? Did either community remain static in a time of flux, or were there continual adaptations that produced the patterns of diversification consistently found among Texans by historians and social scientists? How, in short, did Anglos and Mexicans respond to the changes of the nineteenth century?

To address these questions, we have blended the techniques of historical and sociological research. A note on methodology is fitting at this point. Many primary and secondary sources informed the writing of this book, and we owe a debt to many social historians who have advanced the study of Texas and Mexican-American history. Readers will also notice frequent references to sample data collected and analyzed for this volume. These represent new information that should serve as a valuable resource in themselves.

The data derive from the original manuscript records of the decennial censuses of Texas from 1850 through 1900 (excluding those for 1890, which were destroyed by fire). The data set includes measurements of twenty-five specific characteristics of more than 100,000 Texas residents. The subjects lived during the last half of the nineteenth century in Texas counties selected because of their high concentrations of Mexican-American population. These twenty counties were: Cameron, Duval, Nueces, Starr, and Webb in south Texas; Atascosa, Bee, Bexar, Guadalupe, Karnes, Travis, and Victoria in central Texas; and Crane, Crockett, El Paso, Pecos, Presidio, Sutton, Tom Green, and Val Verde in west Texas. Census takers did not canvass some of the sampled counties for each of the designated census years. In 1850, for example, the rigors of life in west Texas precluded making a census, although several permanent settlements then existed in the El Paso Valley. Furthermore the state did not organize some counties until the 1860s or later; hence the censuses for earlier decades do not incorporate them.

The study employed a random-sampling procedure to select the 101,289 subjects to insure an accurate representation of the actual populations of the sampled counties. The size of a county's enumerated population in a given census year formed the basis of the procedure. Where the population numbered less than 150, sampling included all persons residing in the county (this was the

PREFACE case in Crockett county in 1880 and Crane county in 1900). When the population exceeded 150 but amounted to less than 12,000, records from every fourth page of the county's census report provided a sample of approximately 25 percent. In counties where the population surpassed 12,000 people, the procedure used a formula designed to produce a sample of approximately 3,000 from the census report.[3] Statistical analysis shows that the samples do represent the countywide populations; for example, there are strong correlations (.90 or better) between the age distributions of the various samples and those of the corresponding populations, and there are similarly close associations between the sex and nativity distributions. The sampling procedure, however, did result in one difficulty that requires attention.

Because the procedure allowed for the inclusion of all residents of small counties but established a maximum of some 3,000 residents from larger ones, the samples comprise varying percentages of the actual populations. Indeed these ratios, known as sampling fractions, range from a high of 100 percent to a low of 4 percent. The problem that results from such variations is manifest only when combining countywide samples to develop composite estimates of population characteristics for the south-, central-, and west-Texas regions. Small counties with high sampling fractions then overcontribute to the composite picture, while large counties with small sampling fractions undercontribute. Thus composite estimates require adjustments to increase the contribution of undersampled counties and to reduce the contribution of oversampled counties. Figures reported here incorporate such adjustments.[4]

Finally readers need an explanation of the ethnic labels we employ. Herein, the word *Mexican* means people of Mexican descent, regardless of their place of birth, and we utilize the Spanish translation *Mexicano,* which is a self-referrant, in the same manner. We employ the words *Tejano, Texas Mexican,* and *Mexican Americans* when speaking of the entire community. We identify those whose motherland is Mexico by applying such terms as *immigrants, new arrivals,* or *the foreign-born.* We apply the term *Anglo* to persons of Anglo-American and European descent, and occasionally we use the word *white* in the same way. We use *Anglo Texan* broadly to describe the community as a whole. The word *native Texan* refers to those of Anglo-American or European descent who were born in Texas, and *Anglo immigrant* denotes people who migrated to Texas either from another state in the United States or from Europe. When touching on ethnic groups other than Mexicans or Anglos, we strive to use labels that are both clear and appropriate. Unfortunately such references may not please all readers, but style and convenience dictate the use of some generic labels.

While researching and writing this book, we were assisted and supported by numerous individuals. First and foremost our thanks go to Virginia Losoya and Shelly Cope, who helped in preparing the sample data from the original census reports. Special thanks go to the staff of the Angelo State University Computer Center, who have effectively served our data-processing needs over a long period. Many people have nurtured and encouraged our scholarly interest in this project; foremost among these are H. Dempsey Watkins, John M. Wheeler, and our spouses, Susan W. Carpenter and Dolores De León. To these friends and loved ones, we give our gratitude.

Kenneth L. Stewart
Arnoldo De León
Spring 1992

A
Land
of
New
Beginnings,
1519–1900

Texas has extended a challenge to humankind since time immemorial. Native Americans for thousands of years faced the challenge of adapting to the environment; in the main they succeeded. When Europeans arrived several well-organized tribal societies sustained themselves in settled farming communities in eastern Texas. Along the Gulf Coast and the Río Grande plain, less technologically advanced groups subsisted by hunting and gathering across southern and central Texas. In the plains and prairies of western Texas lived nomadic hunters (after the introduction of the horse) who depended on the roaming buffalo for their food, housing, and clothing.

The Spaniards, who explored and mapped the coastline of modern-day Texas as early as 1519, attempted to turn the vast undeveloped space into a productive colony like those of Latin America. Mexicans followed similar goals after overthrowing Spanish rule in 1821. They sought to organize the province politically and vitalize the region's agrarian and commercial sectors. Following the Texas war for independence in 1836, Anglo Texans also desired progress and pursued it through republicanism and their own brand of economic enterprise.

Most of these civilizations rose, in unique ways, to the challenge of Texas. Anglo-Americans especially have succeeded in realizing their goals during the most recent era of Texas history. Alongside them, however, other ethnic groups have pursued ambitions for social progress and material security. What has happened in this competition between two of the peoples of Texas, the Anglos and the Tejanos, is the subject of this book.

Spanish activity in Texas began at the time the army of Hernán Cortés sought to conquer the Aztecs at Tenochtitlán. In the years following, Spaniards ventured into Texas for various reasons, among them the desire to duplicate the success of fellow *conquistadores* who had found rich kingdoms in Mexico and Peru. When the French threatened the Texas region in the 1680s, the Spanish reacted with dispatch to establish title to the area, charting unexplored land in the process. This effort to repel the French also generated another element of interest in Texas; churchmen wanted to proselytize among the Tejas Indians in east Texas. The initiative for spiritual conversion of the natives met disappointment, however, and no permanent Spanish settlements existed in Texas by the beginning of the eighteenth century (except for those in the El Paso Valley which grew out of designs to colonize New Mexico).[1] Nonetheless the sallies into Texas between 1519 and the 1690s solidified Spanish claims to the territory and produced valuable information about the ethnology and ecology of the region.

Spaniards began considering the province with renewed seriousness in the early eighteenth century, out of a lingering fear of a French movement into Texas from the Mississippi Valley. The viceroy in New Spain (Mexico) thus ordered Captain Domingo Ramón to east Texas in 1716 with an entourage of soldiers, missionaries, lay brothers, and a number of civilian settlers. This expedition implanted the first European settlement near modern-day Nacogdoches. Two years later Martín de Alarcón ventured into Texas with the task of establishing a base more firmly linking the far-off missions of east Texas to New Spain. A settlement called Béxar, along the San Antonio River, resulted. Another campaign in 1721 took possession of the site of La Bahía del Espíritu Santo (moved to its present location near Goliad in 1749).[2]

Those who came in the eighteenth century generally originated in locations in Coahuila and other northeastern states of New Spain.[3] They included *mestizos* (mixed-bloods), settled Indians, and Spaniards (although the Iberians were in the minority). Most were the products of generations of intermixture between Indians and Spaniards, and in the settlements of Texas the biological intermingling continued with Indian converts and other women in the vicinity.[4]

As the population increased through natural reproduction and subsequent immigration from New Spain, the early settlements spread into three ecological regions. In distant east Texas the population centered in the Piney Woods, with its major community being Nacogdoches. In east Texas the Spaniards established missions to convert the sedentary Indians who lived as agriculturists, stationed troops to protect the region from French threats, and founded a ranching economy that flourished by the 1750s.[5] The central-Texas region, situated midway between modern-day east Texas and New Spain proper, consisted of the old settlements of La Bahía and Béxar, as well as numerous ranches lying along the valley of the San Antonio River.[6]

Another population center grew up in modern-day south Texas. Known as part of the "Seno mexicano," the area between the Río Grande and the Nueces River came into the state of Tamaulipas following its settlement in the latter 1740s and 1750s by the indefatigable José de Escandón. To discourage occupation by rival European powers and to stave off Indian attacks on Nuevo León, Escandón established in northern Tamaulipas missions and towns such as Camargo, Reynosa, Revilla, Mier, and Laredo. The region's mild climate and lush vegetation offered an abundance of pasturage for sheep, goats, horses, and cattle; the several settlements prospered.[7]

In far-west Texas lay an area of arid climate and slight vegetation, claimed and settled by the Spaniards but not well populated. There friars in 1682 had founded the first European site in modern Texas, close to the current city of El Paso. Over the years settlers came to live in villages like Ysleta, Socorro, and San Elizario. Despite the region's location in modern-day Texas, however, Spanish authorities in New Mexico administered it.[8]

When Mexico won its independence in 1821, it faced the same concerns in Texas as had the Spaniards: the problems of countering Indian hostility, sustaining missionary work, protecting against foreign imperialism, and domesticating the difficult Texas landscape. The most immediate need was to define the status of Texas within a new constitutional arrangement established in Mexico. In attempting to implement such a political order, architects of the new government adhered to the federalist principles advanced by some of New Spain's postindependence thinkers. Mexico's Constitution of 1824 thus took as its models the United States Constitution and the Spanish Constitution of 1812. The latter document synthesized a Spanish medieval tradition, stressing natural law and placing the interest of the community over that of individuals, with more modern political doctrines and ideals that arose from the Enlightenment.[9] Mexicans borrowed freely from the Spanish Constitution, while adjusting it to meet the needs of the new nation. Significantly they conceded power to provincial interests and granted the states the right to manage their internal affairs.[10] The founders of the new government then merged Texas with the frontier state of Coahuila until the population of the province (about twenty-five hundred in 1821) should increase.[11]

A second important concern for Mexico and the Tejanos was the age-old problem of protecting Texas. Mexico still needed to guard against foreign encroachment in east Texas. The Spanish had experimented with several defensive policies, even to the extent of inviting settlers from the United States to settle in Louisiana, and then, in January 1821, permitting Moses Austin of Missouri to settle Anglo-American families on the Brazos River. When Mexico achieved independence that same year, it chose to follow the precedent. Liberals no longer supported the missions as colonizing institutions, and the country did not have the population to settle the north. Thus Stephen F. Austin was granted the right to assume his recently deceased father's contract, allowing American settlers to people Texas.[12] Other *empresarios* followed as Mexico hoped to use a policy of controlled Anglo settlement as a means of preventing loss of sovereignty over the threatened territory. Obviously the effects of this policy were eventually of extreme importance in determining the destiny of Texas.

A third consideration for Mexico and Texas Mexicans was vitalizing the region's agrarian and commercial capacities. In the colonial period, the crown had granted land to desiring colonizers, and many had engaged in livestock raising.[13] In Texas it was the central and southern regions that lent themselves most readily to ranch operations. In the 1820s and 1830s, Texas abounded with feral range cattle and horses, and *rancheros* in central Texas continued turning to these resources for profit. But the government imposed regulations on branding, slaughtering, trading, taming, and rounding up range animals in an effort to control the enterprise.[14] While the restrictions hampered growth of the industry, landowners nonetheless managed to sell meat locally and even drive their stock to Louisiana and the northern Mexican states below the Río Grande.[15]

In south Texas, horses and cattle (both tame and feral) in the countryside between the Río Grande and the Nueces numbered into the thousands.[16] Since occupying the region, Mexican grantees had been ranching, leaving *vaqueros* to tend to the livestock and returning from the safer settlements along the river to check their holdings as needed. While recurrent Indian attacks forced the *pobladores* (settlers) to withdraw southward periodically, they invariably regrouped, so that by the late 1820s, Mexican rancheros were successfully claiming the territory.[17] The same pattern of expansion was evident in the rural districts around Laredo. In the 1820s *ranchos* offered new job opportunities for poor working people and respectable incomes for men of means.[18]

While the spread of ranchos had been the primary thrust of development in Texas during the colonial era, Tejano leaders looked to foreign immigration as a foundation for ambitious plans to modernize their province. In this visionary plan, Anglos would afford some security from Indians, make the most of the country's natural resources (including cultivating its lands), and organize its commercial potential.[19] The development of the province, they believed, would propel them into a web of economic activity stretching to Louisiana, Coahuila, and even Mexico's far north. Béxar oligarchs lobbied for policies permitting foreigners to use the Gulf ports without payment of customs duties and for laws excluding Anglos from general taxation.[20] They even succeeded in 1828 in having the state legislature allow immigrants to bring slaves into Texas under indenture contracts. These slaves, they thought, would perform the essential tasks needed for setting commercial agriculture in motion.[21]

In the end Mexico's attempts to foster prosperity unwittingly deflected the course of Texas history. The effort to protect the territory and advance its modernization by peopling it with foreigners, though imaginative on the surface, proved particularly fatal to Mexican interests. By the late 1820s, these efforts by the Tejano entrepreneurial element to further the province economically produced alarm. According to Mexican inspectors touring Texas during the era, the Anglos in east Texas communities freely pursued cash-crop farming, commerce, and land speculation, while the Tejano settlements showed little advancement.[22] Fearing a possible drive for self-rule among the newcomers, Mexico sought to block the Anglo influx, although political rivalries in Mexico City forestalled the formulation of any consistent immigration policy. By 1836 the Anglo-American population (primarily from the southern United States) and their slaves numbered about thirty-five thousand. Tejano inhabitants numbered only about thirty-five hundred.[23] The break between the province and Mexico occurred on 21 April 1836, when Texans won their independence at the Battle of San Jacinto.

Now Texans went about the task of establishing an institutional order more in keeping with Anglo-American sentiments of political democracy. In the forty years after 1836, Texas government passed through several stages. It

CHAPTER 1   stood as the Lone Star Republic from 1836 until it joined
the Union in 1845. It existed as an American state until
1861 when it seceded, then remained a part of the Confederacy for the next four years. In rejoining the Union
in 1865, it passed through the several phases of postbellum reconstruction: Conservative Reconstruction between 1866 and 1867, Congressional or Radical Reconstruction from 1867 through 1872, then resumption of
the state's autonomy, starting with the democratic legislative victory of 1872 and culminating in the Constitution
of 1876.

While each of these periods reflected the unique conditions of the times, they were nevertheless all bound
together by a common political tradition. The constitutions of 1836, 1845, 1866, 1869, and 1876 all em-
bodied the traditional American political ethos. These
official documents affirmed the "rights of man" and
other general beliefs of a people steeped in the legacy of
Anglo-American democratic political philosophy. Legal
elements dealing with community property, family relations, and water rights were borrowed from the Spanish-
Mexican heritage, but the state government moved in a
direction based on political thinking originating east of
the Sabine River.

The new governments of Texas, also in the traditional American way, reinforced and gave legitimacy
to ideologies based on color. The negative attitudes of
Anglos toward blacks and Native Americans remained
entrenched in Texas politics for the entire century. The
antebellum constitutions recognized slavery, and while
the Thirteenth Amendment eliminated "the peculiar institution," it did not eradicate racist feelings. Texans continued thinking of African Americans and Indians as sav-
age peoples, unworthy of integration into white society;
by the end of the century, Texas was a stronghold of segregation policies among southern states. Although Tejanos

felt the brunt of legal segregation in a less direct manner than either African Americans or Indians, whites classified them with the other "colored" groups. Thoroughly implicit in the governments after 1836 was the notion that Texas was the home of "white folks."

The racial bent of Anglo Texas politics, abhorred by some and defended by others, never became an issue strong enough to dull the state's attraction for immigrants. With independence won and new governments beckoning newcomers, people looked to Texas for fresh beginnings. No precise count of the number arriving between 1836 and 1900 is available, but the influx was large and accounted for a significant part of the increase in the state's population. Barnes F. Lathrop, in his pioneering study of immigration into east Texas, estimated that more than 2,400 families moved into the area east of the Trinity river between 1836 and 1850.[24] The total population of the state more than quadrupled during that time. Lathrop also estimated that more than 200,000 individuals immigrated to Texas between 1850 and 1860, when the state's population increased nearly threefold.[25] During the last three decades of the century, the population increased almost fourfold again; over 607,000 arrived in Texas during that time, according to Census Bureau estimates.[26] Thus after the Anglo-American takeover, Texas became a magnet on America's frontier of new beginnings. The population increased at a rate almost six times that of the total United States in the last fifty years of the century.[27] Immigrants poured in with dreams of developing the vast acreage, promoting industry, and finding wealth and fortune. From 1836 to 1900, the state's population increased from somewhere between 25,000 and 50,000 to 3,948,710.[28]

The immigrants were a varied lot. Their origins included the United States and its territories, as well as many foreign nations. Among the foreigners, Germans

Table 1 Origins of Texas Immigrants, 1850–1900[a]

Place of Origin	1850 Number	1850 % Total	1900 Number	1900 % Total
Southern United States[b]	77,836	74.4	730,090	71.4
Lower South	(35,543)	(34.0)	(376,175)	(36.8)
Upper South	(42,293)	(40.4)	(353,915)	(34.6)
Other United States[c]	10,057	9.6	112,688	11.0
Germany[d]	8,411	8.0	58,438	5.7
Mexico	4,459	4.3	71,062	7.0
Other Foreign	3,904	3.7	49,857	4.9
Total	104,667	100.0	1,022,135	100.0

[a]Source: *United States Census of Population,* ser. nos. 1850.1–1900.22, twenty-six reels of microfilm holdings of the Social and Economic Statistics Administration Library (Formerly, Bureau of the Census Library), Suitland, Maryland (New Haven: Research Publications, Inc.), 1850.1, pp. xxxvi–xxxvii; 1900.1, pp. clxxiii–xlxxxiv, cxxvi–cxxx.

[b]Southern states of origin are divided into "lower" and "upper" southern states. Included in the lower south are Alabama, Florida, Georgia, Louisiana, Mississippi, and South Carolina. Arkansas, the District of Columbia, Kentucky, Maryland, Missouri, North Carolina, Tennessee, and Virginia (and West Virginia in 1900) are included in the upper south. The distinction between these regions of the south was developed by Terry G. Jordan in "The Imprint of the Upper and Lower South on Mid-Nineteenth Century Texas," *Annals of the Association of American Geographers* 57 (1967) 667–90. Also see Jordan, "Population Origins of Texas, 1850," *The Geographical Review 59* (January 1969) 83–103.

[c]All U.S. states and territories other than those classified in the lower and upper south are included in this category.

[d]People born in Austria, Prussia, and Switzerland are included among those originating in Germany. People listed as Germans from Poland also are included in the 1900 figures.

and Mexicans were most numerous. In combination these two groups comprised about 12 percent of the immigrants in both 1850 and 1900. Other foreigners, primarily from the United Kingdom and other European sources, made up 4 to 5 percent. Of all the immigrants to Texas, however, the largest group consisted of Anglo Americans from the southern United States. In both 1850 and 1900, this group comprised over 70 percent of Texas residents not born in the state (see table 1).

In an excellent investigation of immigration to Texas in the midnineteenth century, the geographer Terry G.

Jordan has shown that upon arriving, immigrants did not settle in a random or mixed fashion.[29] The various groups instead held together and staked out different territories for themselves. By 1850 a series of identifiable ethnic regions had emerged (see map). Of these, three were the most expansive and general. First there was a region in east Texas settled primarily by people from the lower tier of southern states.[30] This area stretched from Harrison, Upshur, and Smith counties in the north to Wharton, Brazoria, and Matagorda counties in the south. It included most of the border with Arkansas and Louisiana and the northernmost half of the Gulf coastline. This area will be called the *lower-southern settlement region.*

A second general region developed along a corridor reaching from the Red River southward to the central-Texas counties of Guadalupe, Gonzales, and Lavaca. Predominantly settled by immigrants from the upper southern states, by 1850 this area formed a wedge of land adjacent to east Texas and the hill country to the west.[31] This will be called the *upper-southern settlement region.* The Germans, who formed the largest single foreign group in 1850, established a fragmented belt of communities cross-cutting the southern portions of the lower and upper southern settlement regions. Inclined more than the Anglo-Americans to settle in towns and cities, about a third of the Germans in 1850 located between Galveston and San Antonio, although others had established enclaves in the state's hill country around Fredericksburg. Their pattern of settlement never really resulted in the emergence of a distinctively German region. Instead clusters of communities arose within the more general and expansive regions of southern Anglo-American settlement.

The flow of Mexican immigration shaped a third general settlement region. Called the *Mexican settlement region,* this area includes some of the most sparsely populated territory in the state, most notably south Texas. Also

11

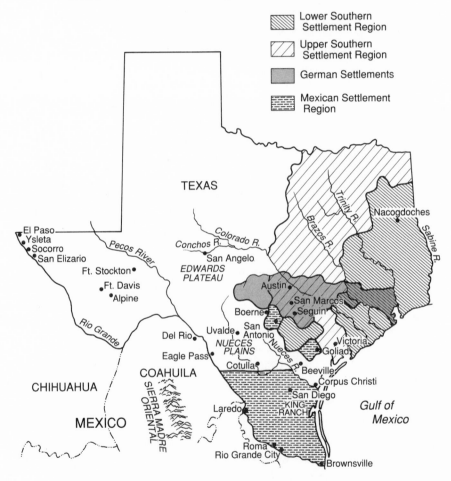

Settlement Areas of Immigrants to Texas, 1850

Legend:
- Lower Southern Settlement Region
- Upper Southern Settlement Region
- German Settlements
- Mexican Settlement Region

TEXAS

Nacogdoches

El Paso
Ysleta
Socorro
San Elizario
Ft. Stockton
Ft. Davis
Alpine

Pecos River

Conchos R.
Colorado R.
San Angelo

EDWARDS PLATEAU

Trinity R.
Brazos R.
Sabine R.

Austin
San Marcos
Boerne
Seguin

Rio Grande

Del Rio
Uvalde
San Antonio

NUECES PLAINS

Victoria
Goliad

Eagle Pass

Cotulla

Beeville

Corpus Christi

CHIHUAHUA

COAHUILA

SIERRA MADRE ORIENTAL

San Diego

Gulf of Mexico

MEXICO

Laredo

KING RANCH

Roma
Rio Grande City

Brownsville

12

included, though less dominated by Mexicans, were a few more densely populated central Texas counties, especially Bexar and Goliad.

By 1900 the areas fed by the major groups of immigrants had expanded greatly. Still their settlement patterns remained separate and distinctive. With the subduing of the Indians and the coming of the railroads, Mexican immigration became the primary source of population for newly formed counties such as Maverick, Val Verde, and Brewster in west Texas along the upper banks of the Río Grande. Anglo-American southerners, on the other hand, made their way by the thousands into the expansive prairies between the hill country and El Paso.

Since the 1820s the immigrants had brought with them the hope of developing Texas by promoting industry and agriculture. Independence in 1836 permitted them the opportunity to put their notion of free enterprise into effect. Difficulty confronted their ambitions at first, for the state remained isolated from the rest of the United States until midcentury, a frontier region without adequate transportation facilities to move commodities. By the 1850s, however, the advances that Mexican inspectors had observed before the war for independence were becoming more pronounced. In the beginning of that decade, over twelve thousand farms were operating in the state, encompassing a land area of about 11.5 million acres. This amounted to 1 percent of all farms and 4 percent of the total farm acreage in the United States.[32] Actually Texas farms were larger than the average across the nation and generally less productive in terms of gross output of major cash crops.[33] Nevertheless the diversity of products from the state's farms in 1850 hinted at its agricultural promise. Beside the more than 57,000 bales of cotton reported for that year, Texas farmers produced over 6.2 million bushels of corn and grain products, 66,000 pounds of tobacco, 1.6 million bushels of garden products, and $1.1 million in slaughtered livestock.[34] While Texas was not a major United States agricultural producer, the incipient development of a commercial farming economy was evident.

Associated with the midcentury advance of agriculture was the emergence of a distinctive economic regionalism. The development of farming did not occur evenly, and the disparities correlated with the general ethnic settlement regions that emerged. Of the three areas, the one centered in east Texas, where immigrants from the lower south dominated the population, led the way in agricultural advancement. The lower-southern settlement region contained over half of the farm acreage in 1850 and produced as much as 70 percent of cash crops. The section occupied primarily by upper southerners lagged slightly behind in the early advance of agriculture, but it was the Mexican region in central and south Texas where development occurred at the slowest pace. In 1850 only about 4 percent of Texas farmland existed there, and the production of some important cash crops (e.g., cotton) was nonexistent (see table 2). Plainly it was the distinctively white ethnic regions of Texas that flourished most under the Anglo-Texan regime.[35]

No event of the last half of the nineteenth century leveled these ethnic regional differences in the Texas economy. In the years immediately following the Civil War, state commerce became integrated into the wider United States markets, even as Texans underwent the divisiveness of Reconstruction politics. By the 1870s Galveston and Houston had emerged as ports of entry for outside goods as well as centers for exporting cotton to northern factories. Dallas was developing into a commercial center in north Texas, with railroad connections to markets outside the state. San Antonio became a military headquarters, the central depot for federal frontier posts, and an eminent frontier center.[36] For Texas the postbellum period

Table 2   Texas Agriculture, 1850[a]

Agricultural Traits	Upper-Southern Settlement Region[b]	% of State Total	Lower-Southern Settlement Region[b]	% of State Total	Mexican Settlement Region[b]	% of State Total
Acres of Farmland	4,687,355	41.1	6,157,357	54.0	479,186	4.2
Improved Acreage	252,863	39.6	376,151	58.9	7,106	1.1
Value of Farms	$4,919,337	30.0	$9,313,687	56.8	$470,080	2.9
Value of Farm Implements & Machinery	$736,234	34.5	$1,346,122	63.1	$24,612	1.2
Value of Slaughtered Livestock	$476,165	43.0	$620,678	56.1	$11,673	1.1
Production of Corn & Grain Products (bushels)	2,557,387	41.1	3,324,480	53.0	123,045	2.0
Production of Cotton (Pounds)	6,836,400	29.7	16,182,000	70.2	——	—
Production of Tobacco (Pounds)	23,514	35.1	43,023	64.3	230	0.3
Production of Garden Products (bushels)	453,881	28.4	1,143,345	71.4	2,629	0.2

[a] Source: *U.S. Census of Population,* 1850.1, pp. 514–20.

[b] Counties were assigned to the settlement regions as follows: the upper-southern settlement region, Anderson, Bastrop, Bowie, Burleson, Caldwell, Calhoun, Cass, Collin, Cooke, Coryell, Dallas, Denton, Ellis, Fannin, Fayette, Gonzales, Grayson, Guadalupe, Hays, Henderson, Hopkins, Hunt, Jackson, Kaufman, Lamar, Limestone, Milam, Navarro, Red River, Robertson, Tarrant, Titus, Travis, Van Zandt, Victoria, Washington, and Williamson counties; lower-southern settlement region, Angelina, Austin, Brazoria, Brazos, Cherokee, Colorado, De Witt, Fort Bend, Galveston, Grimes, Harris, Harrison, Houston, Jasper, San Augustine, Shelby, Smith, Tyler, Upshaw, Walker, and Wharton counties; and the Mexican settlement region, Bexar, Cameron, Goliad, Nueces, Starr, and Webb counties.

was also the era of cattle, and the demand for beef in the North and in the western territories absorbed Texas cattle ranches into the national economy. Ranchmen from south Texas drove their herds to Sedalia, Missouri, or to various railheads in Kansas, while those in the western section of the state took their stock to New Mexico and

Colorado. The booming cattle industry permitted Texans to tap into markets outside the state, including major hubs of industrial activity throughout the country.[37]

With the arrival of railroads during the late 1870s and after, the push toward modernity in Texas accelerated. Iron tracks soon connected previously isolated regions with one another, and the state itself with the Atlantic and Pacific coasts. Railroad lines opened to settlement sparsely populated sections, expanded the urban areas and gave birth to new towns, stimulated the rise of new industries, and opened major new markets throughout the country to commodities such as cotton, lumber, and various other raw materials.[38] Driven by rail-transportation technology, the move toward commercial ranching and farming accelerated, spurring a rapid increase in Texas agricultural productivity. More than 352,000 farms operated in Texas by 1900, nearly thirty times the number in 1850.

Also stimulated by the railroads was a sizable investment in various manufacturing enterprises and the growth of a notable, though not dominant, industrial sector in the state's economy. Some 12,000 manufacturing establishments, operating on capital investments totaling more than $90 million and producing over $119 million in products were present in Texas by the turn of the century.[39] Enterprises included lumber milling, cottonseed milling, flour milling, cotton ginning and compressing, train and railroad repairing, liquor brewing, and meat packing, to name a few.[40]

All the economic growth in late-nineteenth-century Texas, however, did little to change the pattern of ethnic and regional inequality that had solidified earlier. The primary effect of the process of modernization was to shift the dominant locus of production from the lower-southern settlement area to the upper-southern region.

The Mexican settlement region, continued to trail in economic development, as it had in 1850.

At midcentury little more than seven thousand acres of improved farmland existed in the Mexican settlement region. This amounted to only 1.1 percent of the state's total improved farm acreage. On this land the region's farmers and ranchers produced only 1.1 percent of the state's total value of livestock products, 2.0 percent of the corn and grain yield, and less than 1.0 percent of the tobacco and garden product output (see table 2). By 1900 improved farmland in the Mexican region increased to over 646,000 acres, but this still only amounted to 3.3 percent of the statewide total. Farm output climbed, and the region produced 4.4 percent of the states's nonlivestock farm yield and nearly 14.0 percent of the livestock value (see table 3). But while agricultural productivity in the Mexican region kept pace with, or outpaced, that of other regions, investment and improvement in its farm and ranch operations lagged.

The same geographic disparity existed in industrial development. The Mexican settlement region attracted only 11 percent of the $90 million capital investment in Texas manufacturing operations in 1900 while producing 14.3 percent of the value of manufactured products. In comparison the upper-southern settlement region, the state's dominant production area by 1900, netted 33.1 percent of total capital investment in manufacturing and produced 39.2 percent of the product value (see table 4). Although business in the Mexican region proved profitable and the productivity of labor compared favorably with other sections of the state, developers and investors continued to prefer other regions. The net effect of economic expansion in Texas was to reproduce inequality among regions on a grander scale.

During the nineteenth century, Tejanos and Anglos

Table 3   Texas Agriculture, 1900[a]

Agricultural Traits	Upper-Southern Settlement Region[b]	% of State Total	Lower-Southern Settlement Region[b]	% of State Total	Mexican Settlement Region[c]	% of State Total
Number of Farms	146,643	41.6	74,633	21.2	11,098	3.2
Acres of Farmland	16,009,255	12.7	9,552,426	7.6	25,967,614	20.6
Improved Acreage	7,873,473	40.2	3,129,394	16.0	646,306	3.3
Value of Farms	$227,927,715	38.5	$64,474,350	10.9	$57,359,352	9.7
Value of Farm Buildings	$56,158,057	56.0	$16,298,681	16.2	$4,465,920	4.5
Value of Farm Implements & Machinery	$13,860,210	46.0	$4,547,920	15.1	$4,127,240	3.7
Value of Livestock	$54,334,078	22.6	$22,736,549	9.5	$32,351,074	13.5
Value of Nonlivestock	$93,653,133	44.7	$31,891,888	15.2	$9,300,344	4.4

[a]Source: *U.S. Census of Population*, 1900. 4–5, Report 229, pp. 4–6. Percents in table 3 will not total 100 because the three regions do not cover the entire state. (For example, none of the Panhandle is included in the three regions. Thus the regions cover only 66 percent of total farms, 40.9 percent of total farm acreage, and 59.5 percent of improved acres.)

[b]The upper and lower southern settlement regions are the same as those represented in table 2.

[c]The 1900 Mexican settlement region here includes the counties noted in table 2 plus Atascosa, Bee, Brewster, Crane, Crockett, Duval, El Paso, Hidalgo, Jeff Davis, Karnes, Kinney, Maverick, Pecos, Presidio, Sutton, Tom Green, Val Verde, Victoria, and Zapata counties. This list almost corresponds to that of counties selected for sampling individual residents of the Mexican settlement region. The differences are as follows: Guadalupe and Travis counties are included in our sample data, but are incorporated here in the figures for the upper-southern settlement region; and Brewster, Hidalgo, Jeff Davis, Kinney, Maverick, and Zapata counties are included in these calculations for the Mexican settlement region but do not appear in the sample data. The sample data will be cited throughout the book as a basis for estimating various population characteristics and trends in the Mexican settlement region.

sought to develop a stable society. Early in the century Tejanos directed the effort to modernize the economy and to establish a political system founded on democratic ideals. Eventually Anglo Americans mounted a successful campaign for independence from Mexico. They then replaced the Spanish-Mexican system with a government reflecting American republicanism and Anglo ways of thinking that included racial assumptions about the in-

Table 4 Texas Industry, 1900[a]

Industrial Traits	Upper-Southern Settlement Region[b]	% of State Total	Lower-Southern Settlement Region[b]	% of State Total	Mexican Settlement Region[b]	% of State Total
Number of Establishments	5,120	41.7	2,630	21.4	822	6.7
Invested Capital	$29,922,568	33.1	$31,434,431	34.8	$9,960,735	11.0
Number of Wage Earners[c]	17,092	35.5	15,446	32.1	9,978	20.6
Total Wages	$7,016,746	34.1	$6,342,748	30.9	$3,107,717	15.1
Value of Products	$46,788,227	39.2	$34,067,798	28.5	$17,110,965	14.3

[a] Source: *U.S. Census of Population,* 1900.4–3, Report 146, pp. 10–15.

[b] Counties were assigned to the settlement regions in the manner described in table 3.

[c] Average number of wage earners employed per day over a twelve-month period.

feriority of "colored" people such as Tejanos. By mid-century advancements in agriculture and, by the 1870s, in the industrial sector began taking Texas toward an age of modernity. Regional economic inequality based on patterns of ethnic settlement accompanied this shift. In the process of modernization, Anglos had become dominant; Tejanos were subordinated.

Laborers and Regional Economic Disparities

Of the changes that swept the state from 1850 to 1900, none is more salient than the economic transformation. The number of farms shot up remarkably, as 12,000 operating enterprises in 1850 increased by 340,000 by the turn of the century. Of these additional farming ventures, 86 percent began operations in the 1870s or later. Similarly large increases in farm acreage, manufacturing establishments, and annual dollar values of both farm and manufactured products came in the decades after the Civil War.[1]

The most significant human

Table 5   Classification of Gainful Workers in Texas, 1850–1900

Classification	1850	1860	1870	1880	1900	% Gain or Decline
Agriculture	83.7%	60.1%	70.3%	68.8%	62.4%	−21.3%
Professional Service	2.4%	10.0%	11.2%	9.4%	11.5%	+9.1%
Trade and Transportation	4.4%	8.5%	5.7%	6.7%	10.7%	+6.3%
Manufacturing and Mechanical	9.6%	9.3%	6.7%	5.8%	7.8%	−1.8%
Unspecialized	0.0%	12.2%	6.1%	9.2%	7.7%	+7.7%
Total Sample of Workers	30,133	104,031	237,126	522,133	1,033,033	+3328%

Source: Reports from *U.S. Census of Population,* 1850.1, p. 513; 1850.2, p. 128; 1860.2, pp. 490–91; 1870.1, pp. 670–71; 1880.1, pp. 712–13; 1890.2, pp. 302–3; and 1900.18, pp. 392–97. Figures for 1850 and 1860 include only the free male population over fifteen years of age. Figures for 1870–1900 include all gainful workers over ten years of age. The classification system is based on that employed by the Census Bureau in 1870. Adjustments were made in the 1880–1900 figures due to the bureau's reclassification of certain occupations.

aspect of this transition toward modernity was a pronounced redistribution of employment opportunities in the state and within its various regions (see table 5). With improvements in transportation and other technologies, new markets for Texas commodities opened. In turn the proportion of workers committed to the agricultural sector decreased, while the percentage involved in service, trade, transportation, manufacture, and unspecialized labor pursuits increased. In short a proportionate displacement of agricultural labor occurred as both demands and opportunities changed for workers with differing skills.

These changes in labor markets acted to the benefit of Anglo Texans and to the detriment of Tejanos as both competed for material advancement. Anglo workers profited perceptibly from the new opportunities. To be sure the redistribution of labor also yielded improvements in the status of many Tejano workers, but collectively *obreros* bore a heavier burden of shifting labor demands and economic expansion in late-nineteenth-century Texas. Why was this so? What came to be the occupational status of Tejanos in the context of changing employment opportunities? What historical forces explain why the majority of Tejanos became locked in a particular niche in the new occupational structure? This chapter pursues answers to these questions.

The Mexican settlement region, initially consisting of the southern to central portions of the state and spreading later into west Texas along the upper banks of the Río Grande, shared in the benefits of economic growth, but this area of the state was the last and least advantaged. Real financial animation of investment in the state's nascent industries occurred in those parts of the state more immediately tied to the greater economy of the United States. Similarly small-scale manufacturing enterprises were most likely to crop up where convenient transportation existed for the wider distribution of goods. Thus residence in a part of the state less likely to attract capital investment and many employment opportunities denied Tejanos full participation in the economic boom.[2] Economic expansion failed to level regional economic disparities. As the growth of the economy was itself uneven in regional terms, so were its effects on the distribution of employment opportunities.[3]

The Mexican settlement region, unlike the rest of the state, did not undergo a significant decline in the proportion of its labor force committed to agricultural pursuits (see Table 5 and 6). Where the statewide percentage of agricultural workers dropped by 21.3 percent between 1850 and 1900, the proportion in the Mexican settlement region steadily remained between 24 and 31 percent. Pastoral endeavors never composed as large a segment of the total demand for labor in this region as they did in the state as a whole. Thus the area did not experience the shift

Table 6 Classification of Gainful Workers
in the Mexican Settlement Region, 1850–1900

Classification	1850	1860	1870	1880	1900	% Gain or Decline
Agriculture	24.0%	30.1%	26.2%	31.3%	24.7%	+0.7%
Professional Service	30.6%	21.6%	21.5%	20.2%	16.2%	−14.4%
Trade and Transportation	21.4%	14.7%	10.1%	10.5%	12.7%	−8.7%
Manufacturing and Mechanical	23.7%	13.1%	10.1%	8.2%	9.7%	−14.0%
Unspecialized	0.2%	20.5%	32.1%	29.8%	36.7%	+36.5%
Total Sample of Workers	1,158	3,903	5,740	9,012	13,435	+1060%

Source: Sample data from Atascosa, Bee, Bexar, Cameron, Crane, Crockett, Duval, El Paso, Guadalupe, Karnes, Nueces, Pecos, Presidio, Starr, Sutton, Tom Green, Travis, Val Verde, Victoria, and Webb counties. These figures have been adjusted to account for variations in sampling fractions (see Preface).

of employment from agriculture to other labor sectors of the burgeoning economy.

On the other hand, employment opportunities in the Mexican region were not immune to change. It is ironic that the growth of manufacturing enterprises resulted in a proportionate decline of demand for workers specialized in the manufacture of commodities.[4] This was true to a slight degree for the entire state, but was exacerbated in the Mexican portion, where the percentage of laborers engaged in manufacturing and mechanical occupations dwindled from about 24 percent to 10 percent between 1850 and 1900. Since industrial manufacturing establishments eventually replaced the many home-based industries such as flour mills, meat-packing operations, and sulfur works that had cropped up around the state in the days of its less-commercialized economy, and since the southern area was more self-sufficient and reliant on home enterprises at midcentury, the decline in this category was more drastic in the Mexican region.[5] Its effect on Tejanos was profound.

The penetration of railroads into the once self-supporting economy of the Mexican region created yet another notable shift in the distribution of gainful employments. Before the Civil War and the subsequent coming of the iron horse, transportation to and from the frontiers of south and west Texas had been a rigorous affair, demanding the skill, fortitude, and bravery of many *arrieros* (drivers). The task absorbed a considerable portion of the labor effort, especially in central Texas around San Antonio, which served as the transportation terminus. A full 25 percent of the Bexar County labor force worked as wagon drivers, cartmen, teamsters, and in other transport-related endeavors in 1850. The status of transportation, moreover, meant that merchant enterprises stayed localized and numerous through the region. As the railroad reached the frontiers, however, the demand for those with skill in horse- or ox-drawn transportation was all but eliminated, and merchandising enterprises tended to cluster nearer the steel rails or wither away. The representation of trade and transportation workers fell accordingly. In 1850 about one-fifth (21.4 percent) of the region's workers engaged in such pursuits. By 1900 only about one-eighth (12.7 percent) worked in trade and transportation jobs.[6]

Another shrinking category of work was that of professional and personal service. This group dwindled from about 30.6 percent of the labor force in 1850 to only 16.2 percent in 1900. In actuality this net downturn resulted from a severe decrease in certain jobs and a notable increase in others. In the early decades, professional people accounted for the bulk of the service workers. South Texas was then a territory only recently acquired by the United States, and Native Americans still inhabited west Texas, except for the El Paso Valley. A sizable influx of government officials and agents, military personnel, and other public servants had come to the south and central portions of the state in response to these frontier conditions. The Civil War, Reconstruction, and Indian campaigns kept a large contingent of professionals in the region until the 1880s, but their numbers declined as the political climate became more settled. At the same time, demand for personal-service workers such as laundrymen, waiters, and cooks increased with more transportation and expanded trade between the frontier and the rest of the state.[7] As opportunities for professional employment in the region fell sharply, an increase in personal-service work took up some slack.

The impact of economic transformation on occupations in the Mexican region, then, was distinct. Labor in the state as a whole shifted from the agricultural sector to the service, trade, transportation, and unspecialized segments. Something approaching the reverse was true in the Mexican region, where declining opportunities were concentrated not in agriculture, but in the other specialized labor categories; the number of workers engaged in service, trade, transport, and manufacturing fell by over 35 percent between 1850 and 1900. Since demand for specialized agricultural labor neither increased nor decreased significantly, an extremely large number of workers turned for a living to unspecialized or general-labor pursuits. The shift in this region was not from agriculture to commercial and industrial specializations; rather it was from specialized, skilled occupations to unspecialized, unskilled ones. In this sense the workers of the Mexican settlement region paid a higher price than their counterparts in other parts of the state. By 1900 more than a third (36.7 percent) of them, almost five times the statewide rate, worked at general labor.

Table 7   Classification of Tejano and Anglo Gainful Workers
in the Mexican Settlement Region, 1850–1900

	Tejanos		Anglos	
Classification	1850	1900	1850	1900
Agriculture	41.1%	18.9%	18.1%	32.3%
Professional and Personal Service	0.6%	11.0%	45.1%	16.3%
Trade and Transportation	22.7%	7.6%	17.5%	20.2%
Manufacturing and Mechanical	35.3%	8.0%	19.1%	12.3%
Unspecialized	0.3%	54.5%	0.1%	19.0%
Sample Size	345	7,041	719	5,044

Source: The 1850 figures are based on sample data from the south- and central-Texas counties of Bexar, Cameron, Guadalupe, Nueces, Starr, Travis, Victoria, and Webb. The percentages for 1900 include sample data from a number of additional counties in south, central, and west Texas, including Atascosa, Bee, Crane, Crockett, Duval, El Paso, Karnes, Pecos, Presidio, Sutton, Tom Green, and Val Verde. All percentages have been adjusted to account for variations in sampling fractions (see Preface).

The effects of this historic transformation of the Texas economy were not only disparate by region; they were also ethnically discriminatory. Mexican obreros paid a higher toll than did Anglo workers. As openings in the specialized labor segments became more restricted, opportunities for Tejano participation increasingly dwindled (see table 7). For example, where available jobs in manufacture and mechanical pursuits regionally declined by 14.0 percent between 1850 and 1900, the proportion of Tejanos so employed dropped by 27.3 percent. The number of Anglo workers in the same category fell by only 6.8 percent over the same period. Anglo employment was similarly less effected by the regional decay of opportunities in trade, transportation, and agriculture. In fact white participation in the agrarian sector actually increased by 14.2 percent, and since this segment was not expanding in the region, increasing Anglo involvement meant a corresponding decrease in chances for Tejanos to sustain themselves in farming. Only 18.9 percent of obreros engaged in specialized agricultural occupations in 1900, a decline of 22.2 percent from 1850.[8]

It was the service occupations and unspecialized-labor pursuits that became the designated jobs for Tejanos in the last decades of the nineteenth century. In 1900 these two categories comprised 65.5 percent of all Tejano workers in the Mexican settlement region. Less than 1 percent had worked in the same sectors fifty years earlier. Thus service and general-labor endeavors became a frequent source of employment for Tejanos as the Texas economy transformed. This was true especially of the general-labor group that grew from a negligible proportion of obreros in 1850 to over half in 1900. But the service sector was hardly different. From the standpoint of required skill levels, the work that was open to Mexican Americans in the service sector had much in common with unspecialized, general-labor pursuits. It was the personal service side of the category that offered expanding opportunities; professional employments were disappearing as the necessity and demand for government personnel faded in the closing decades of the century. When the service sector opened to Tejanos, then, it was personal service jobs, not professional opportunities, that became available.[9]

To say that service and general-labor roles became the "niche" of Tejanos in the Mexican settlement region is to say that they became an ephemeral, unskilled working underclass. As demand for skilled labor waned, Anglo workers dominated the available supply of specialized occupations in agriculture, the professions, trade, transportation, and manufacturing. Tejanos, on the other hand, fended for themselves in unspecialized day labor and in a variety of menial, personal-servant capacities.[10]

Why Tejanos did not escape such a condition has long been a topic of discussion among historians. According

to the scenario sketched in the recent historical literature, Anglos brought large amounts of investment capital
with their institutions and culture to the newly conquered
region and then reserved the better occupations for themselves. Under the economic dominance of whites, Mexicanos performed the more menial tasks. Indeed primary
accounts of attitudes toward Mexicans indicate that out
of the process of change there emerged a willful intent to
discriminate against Mexicans in employment.[11] According to one Corpus Christi resident, for instance, Mexicans
were a necessary element in the Nueces area because no
others were available to fill the demand for servants. If
Mexicans were meant for anything, claimed a sheepraiser
from Pleasanton, it was for sheepherding. One of the at-
tractive features of south Texas, advertisers kept saying,
was its abundance of cheap Mexican labor.[12] Institutional
arrangements in the Mexican region, therefore, motivated
Anglos to arrogate certain occupations for themselves
and designate others for Mexicans. "Mexican work" included cotton picking, grubbing, sheepherding, working
cattle, laundry work, food service, and other low-grade
tasks. Positions in the incipient industries and the more
rewarding occupational categories were for white people.

Surely Mexicans were aware of these circumstances
and understood the limits of their prospects. But if that
were the case, then why did they not migrate to sections of the state offering greater job possibilities? Judging
from Chicano history, Mexicanos have always pursued
opportunities, wherever the location. They have traveled
thousands of miles and withstood harsh discrimination,
prejudice, and violence in the effort to feed, cloth, and
house their families. Logically Mexicans should have migrated to eastern or northern Texas, where opportunities
seemed better.

A number of characteristics of the social landscape of
nineteenth-century Texas probably countered any attrac-

tions that portions of the state outside the Mexican region might have had for Tejanos.[13] To begin with, employers in south, central, and western Texas sought obreros of Mexican descent, even though they cast them in a definite role. No equivalent calls for Mexican labor originated in other parts of the state. East- and north-Texas communities were successful enough either in soliciting white emigrants from elsewhere in the United States and Europe or in using the local black population to attend to their labor needs. Tejanos were thus not beckoned to the lower-southern or upper-southern settlement regions, at least not until the 1890s, when landowners in the black-prairie area of central Texas around Caldwell County began seeking Mexican laborers. When the call for workers went out, either because landowners thought they could pay Mexicans less, thought them more tractable workers, or because labor shortages slowed development in the industrializing cities of north and east Texas, Mexicanos then responded quickly.[14] By the early 1900s, viable Mexican-American settlements had become evident in such cities as Houston, Dallas, and Fort Worth, among others.[15]

The pattern of sharecropping that developed in the other regions, especially the eastern part of Texas, probably also served as a deterrent to any sizable Mexican-American influx until the early calls of the 1890s. Although sharecroppers and tenants were a mix of Anglos and blacks, many of them post–Civil War migrants, sharecropping arrangements revolved around old racial distinctions, through which whites in the eastern region molded a pliant African-American labor force. Mexicans must have been wary of penetrating parts of the state where another discriminatory system of labor-market relations already existed.

Probably the most influential factor in Mexican reluctance to migrate in great numbers was the reality that Anglos let it be known, until the 1890s and early twen-

tieth century, that other parts of the state scorned them.
That attitude had deep roots in the history of areas north
of the Mexican region. Immediately after 1836, for example, whites in those areas suspected many Tejanos of
complicity with Santa Anna and expelled them from their
homes in retaliation for the "atrocities" of the Mexican Army. In the 1850s communities along the northern fringes of the Mexican settlement region, specifically
Austin, Goliad, and Seguin, had banished Tejanos from
their homes in the belief that they were aiding slaves
escaping to Mexico. In many other areas close to slave
plantations in those antebellum years, Mexicans were for-
bidden on penalty of death. Interestingly these events took
place at locations in the interstice, where the Mexican
region touched those areas populated by white people,
most of whom had migrated in an earlier era from the
upper- and lower-southern states.[16]

Through the 1880s, then, Anglos in the lower- and
upper-southern settlement regions made it plain that
Mexicans were not welcome. The decided preference was
for workers from the northern states or from Europe,
especially Germany. In 1878, for example, the Dallas
Weekly Herald applauded the arrival of forty-six Germans, saying, "To this class of immigrants, Texas extends
a hearty welcome, and offers inducements that are not
equaled in any other state in the union."[17] Meanwhile the
new pattern of using Mexican labor to replace Anglo tenants aggravated white-supremacist attitudes among Texans threatened by displacement. In 1897 and 1898, White
Cappers from Hays County warned planters not to rent
to Mexicans or blacks, while landlords in Wilson, Gonzales, and DeWitt counties similarly felt pressure to dis-
charge obreros and run off Mexican renters.[18] Mexicanos
remained concentrated in a section of the state where they
occupied the lower levels of an ethnically stratified labor
hierarchy. The consequences were far-reaching.

An important effect of the discriminatory labor structure that emerged in Texas's Mexican settlement region
was the socioeconomic inequality it generated. The Anglo
population of the region, considered collectively, experienced improved chances for bettering their lives as a result
of the sweeping economic transformation. For Tejanos
the opposite was true; they suffered a diminution of the
dreams that attracted them to the Texas frontier. As the
new labor system developed, they lost crucial resources
for improving the conditions of their lives.

Occupations are a primary means of acquiring and
accumulating wage and wealth benefits. Those benefits
serve, in turn, as resources for building a better future.
Since shifting labor demands adversely affected Tejanos,
they experienced a loss of standing both in terms of benefits acquired and accumulated, and most importantly, in
terms of resources available for ameliorating their situation. Several different inquiries into the outcome of disparate ethnic participation in the labor force show that
Tejanos indeed lost ground in their ability to help themselves.

Evidence provided by the Bureau of the Census in two
separate studies, conducted in 1890 and 1900, suggests
that as Mexicans moved progressively into the personal-
servant and general-labor sectors, they became more susceptible to periodic layoffs and job dismissals.[19] The Bureau's first study of unemployment shows that of 696,208
gainful workers in Texas, 74,072, or 10.6 percent, experienced periods of joblessness ranging from one to twelve
months in 1890. Ten years later the Bureau found that
244,828, or 23.7 percent of the state's 1,033,033 workers,
went through unemployment periods of the same dura-
tion. Ominously the occupations most vulnerable to the
downswing of employment were the ones frequently filled
by Tejanos in the Mexican settlement region. In 1900
the region's unspecialized labor group was 73 percent

Mexican, and according to the study of statewide unemployment, this category led the way, with 44.5 percent of its members being out of work for periods of from one month to a year. Personal-service labor also attracted its share of Mexican workers in 1900; 48 percent of laborers in this category were Tejanos in that year. The statewide level of unemployment for service workers was 30.9 percent. The 1900 unemployment levels in the more-skilled occupational classes dominated by Anglos were 25.2 percent for agriculture, 29.3 percent in the professions, 11.9 percent for trade and transportation, and 25 percent for manufacturing and mechanical pursuits. Those occupational spheres where Tejanos worked provided the least opportunity for holding down jobs. This, in turn, hampered their collective capacity to accrue resources for social and economic betterment.

Further investigation of the benefits yielded by occupations suggests that the financial resources available to Tejanos were modest. Concentrated in unspecialized and personal-service endeavors, most obreros were simply part of the available pool of general day laborers hired by farmers, tradesmen, and early industrialists in the Mexican region. According to a report published in 1901 by the United States Industrial Commission, the wages of day laborers on Texas farms declined by about 30 percent between 1866 and 1899. The daily rate for a farm laborer during the harvest season of 1866 amounted to $1.65. By 1899 this had declined to $1.16.[20] Thus an average day laborer fortunate enough to have stayed employed as a farmhand for a thirty-day period would have earned a monthly wage of $49.50 in 1866 and only $34.80 in 1900. Yet these figures may still not reflect reality, because indications are that the cost of living among farm laborers increased as their wages declined.[21] Moreover the average daily wage for farmworkers as a whole may well have exceeded the going rate for Mexicans. Other sources put the wage for Mexican farm- and ranchhands in 1900 at 50 cents per day.[22]

Available information on earnings in manufacturing, on the other hand, shows that workers in this realm, while not above farmhands in absolute monthly wage levels, nonetheless benefited from developments in the last decades of the century.[23] The average monthly earnings of these wage employees in 1870, for example, were $18.80, $30.70 below that of a daily farmhand in 1866. By 1900, however, wage laborers in manufacturing establishments were averaging $35.57 per month, 77 cents more than the average farm worker in 1899. In other words while wages of general laborers in farming fell by 30 percent, the monthly earnings of manufacturing employees increased by 89.2 percent.[24] Since these rates included those of unskilled day workers in manufacturing establishments, the increase for more skilled workers, who more likely were from the Anglo population in the Mexican region, was probably greater, and their wage levels were undoubtedly higher.[25] Salaried workers, furthermore, were earning about $75.59 per month in Texas manufacturing establishments as the century ended.[26] Almost all these employees were Anglos, and their earnings were 113 percent more than those of wage workers in manufacturing, 117 percent higher than laborers in farming.

Statistics of wealth from the decennial censuses between 1850 and 1870 indicate even more firmly that labor inequities severely damaged the ability of Tejanos to command the financial resources necessary for investment in the future.[27] As population spread to the south and west during this twenty-year period, the numbers of both labor groups multiplied, as did their accumulated wealth. But as this occurred, inequalities in wealth distribution between Tejano and Anglo working people intensified.

In 1850 the apportionment of wealth was in fact quite level. Mexicanos comprised 28.9 percent of the total labor force of the region at that time, and about 33 percent of the wealth held by gainful workers was in their hands.[28] The average sum per worker within the Tejano group was $926. Anglos, on the other hand, made up about 62.1 percent of the total number of workers and held some 66 percent of the wealth. The average sum per Anglo worker was $899. By 1870 this situation of approximate parity had eroded. The Mexican working population had expanded to 37.8 percent of the regional labor force, but only 10 percent of the accumulated wealth was in their possession; the average amount per obrero had shrunk to merely $122. Anglo representation in the labor pool declined in the twenty-year period to just 41.7 percent, but they controlled 89 percent of the wealth in 1870; the average accumulation among working Anglos had increased to $942.

The diminishing access Mexicanos had to the fruits of economic change in nineteenth-century Texas also resulted in a transformation of household employment patterns. The late-nineteenth-century Tejano household was usually a patrimonial nuclear family.[29] The majority of men, women, and children lived in households headed by males with only the spouse and children in residence. Most important to the present consideration, however, is that male heads of families dominated the Tejano labor force of 1850. About 70 percent of the laboring population conformed to this pattern, while working spouses and children made up only 19 percent of laborers. By 1900 these numbers had changed. Male heads of families then comprised only 56 percent of working Tejanos, and spouses and children accounted for 26 percent. Over the fifty-year period, the number of working spouses in Mexican families increased from 2.6 percent to 3.7 percent. Even more dramatically, child laborers increased from 4 percent to 16 percent of all children.[30] As the ethnically stratified labor structure evolved, more women

35

and children entered the employment pool to help make ends meet.

The result meant reduced opportunities for the young, in particular, to acquire basic skills to improve the condition of future generations. Chances for formal education became elusive. In 1850, for example, about 7 percent of Mexicanos below the age of twenty-one and pursuing gainful work had attended school within a year of the taking of the census. This proportion dropped to just 2 percent by 1900. The reverse situation existed among Anglos. Only about 1 percent of Anglo minors in the work force had attended school in 1850; 17 percent had in 1900.

All in all economic forces were instrumental in relegating the vast majority of nineteenth-century Tejanos to the bottom rung of society. During the latter half of that century, in Texas, as in so many other areas of the nation, the economy crossed the hump from one of subsistence to an enterprise oriented to the ethos of commercial and industrial capitalism. Both agriculture and industry expanded significantly, but opportunities, though plentiful, were not without limit.

The specific circumstances of economic growth crushed Tejanos' access to new opportunity and deterred them from achievements comparable to those of Anglo Texans. Mexicanos lived in the least-penetrable region of the state. In the earliest years of ensuing economic expansion, they lived in a land of manifest frontier conditions, forbidding enough to enterprising entrepreneurs. Not only was transportation a slow and laborious matter under the inclement conditions in these parts, but prospective commercial expeditions had to hazard the potential for hostility from the Native Americans. Thus the Mexican region of settlement was last to feel the effects of the new economics, and when change arrived, orbits of finance and trade dominated by Anglos in other parts of the state quickly absorbed the area. No focus of economic control lay within the indigenous Mexican population or area of settlement. Even in San Antonio, as much an economic center as there was in the Mexican region, Anglo control over business and trade surpassed that of Texas Mexicans. In consequence, the effect of growth on the occupational structure of the Mexican region was far different from that experienced by workers in other Texas regions. Elsewhere jobs in agriculture gave way to increased opportunities in the professions, trade, transportation, and manufacturing. But in the Mexican area the thrust of the shift was from specialized, skilled occupations to general labor and service work.

Combined with the structural circumstances that worked to exclude Tejanos from the advantages of economic change was the emergence of a racial ideology that pointed toward separation and control. Anglos perceived Mexicans to be the group best suited to the growing demand for menial labor, while whites served as "more fitting" candidates for skilled and professional jobs. Prejudicial sentiment further worked to limit Tejano migration to other parts of the state, where better job prospects might have existed. As might be expected, confinement to low-level, dead-end jobs dashed Tejano chances for a better collective future.

The transformation of the latter half of the nineteenth century was not without its repercussions. Because of economic and technological change, many Tejanos and Anglos faced transitions and adaptations in their ways of life as work opportunities and experiences were reshaped. Significantly Anglo Americans derived more advantage from the change than did Tejanos. Still it is important to maintain a historical perspective on the transition toward modernity in this period.

Regionally the change moved forward at different rates. Centered largely in areas other than the Mexican settlement region, economic change in the northern and eastern portions of Texas was structurally deeper, with more sweeping results. Within the Mexican settlement region, central Texas was most affected, while the southern and western parts felt change only more distantly. Accordingly Professor David Montejano's acclaimed ethnographic study of south Texas shows how the regional traditions of life along the border remained relatively intact, compared to the more jolting changes taking place north of the Nueces. Even in this most sedentary area, however, Montejano's work exposes the importance of shifts toward commercialization in agriculture and cattle raising, transfers in landownership, the rise of an Anglo-American mercantile elite, and the increasing weight of urban centers in the regional economic and political processes of south Texas.[31] In the late nineteenth century, the transition toward modernity was not the uprooting force it was to become later, but its inexorable reformulation of the Texas economic base was among the definitive influences shaping the patterns of Tejano and Anglo-Texan community life as the state made its entry into the twentieth century. The Anglo community controlled the transition, erecting an economic order that left them poised for greater gain. Chances for Tejanos to share equally in further modernization were impaired.

Politics: Challenges and Responses

Political change was as much a part of the transition toward modernity as the transformation of the economy. The acceleration of immigration from the United States, Europe, and Mexico; the rise of larger cities and the incorporation of their commerce into the United States economic orbit; the extension of the railroads into previously remote sections of the state; and the conversion to commercial farming in the 1870s and 1880s all gained approval from voters who saw these changes as signs of progress.

Such developments also negatively affected certain Texas population segments. Within mainstream society, some groups railed against the banes of the new dynamics, among them the problems of monopolies and tenant farming. By the 1880s farmer alliances, third parties, and reform Democrats were campaigning for government action in behalf of disaffected Texans. Politicians responded to an extent, as the 1890s and the early decades of the twentieth century became a time of progressive reform. As a minority Tejanos encountered difficulties in the face of changing conditions. Politically, how did they cope?

Political scientists and other scholars have proposed answers. An early article on the subject was one by Alfredo Cuellar, published in 1970 at a time of heightened demand by Mexican-American students for relevant and objective studies about Chicanos.[1] Cuellar was a Chicano and trained political scientist, ostensibly qualified to interpret the history of Mexican-American politics with impartiality and understanding. His work represented a major contribution as a corrective against alleged Anglo misrepresentation of Chicano political history.[2]

Cuellar aimed in his article to provide a historical background for the more "activist" style of Chicano political participation that emerged in the late 1960s and early 1970s. He conceived the Mexican-American experience in evolutionary terms, describing four basic eras of Chicano politics. Severely handicapped by a lack of well-researched scholarly works, Cuellar portrayed the first period as "apolitical." This phase, which Cuellar claimed characterizes events from the middle of the nineteenth century through the early decades of the twentieth, was a time when two basic trends played out in Mexican-American political activity. Violence and disorder, as exemplified by the Juan N. Cortina War along the Texas border in 1859, were dominant themes between the late

1840s and the mid-1870s. According to Cuellar, this was the natural aftermath of the Mexican War, a struggle to consolidate a conquered people into a new regime. The eventual result of the conflict was retreat and acquiescence by Chicanos.

Conventional political activity marked phase two (ca. 1920–40) according to Cuellar. The theme during this time was to accommodate to the demands of an Anglo-controlled political process. A period of "urban aggressiveness" then followed in the 1940s and 1950s. During this era Chicanos purportedly became full participants in politics under the leadership of Anglos in the urban setting. Finally there surfaced independent "radicalism," which Cuellar saw developing at the time of his writing.

More recently David Montejano has produced a contrasting theme. He argues that Tejanos in south Texas dealt with the transformation by accepting a "peace structure." As Professor Montejano explains, Anglo ranchers arriving in the 1850s adapted themselves imaginatively to local Mexican society by adopting, among other things, the manner in which the old Tejano landowners ruled over the people. Through this accommodationist arrangement, Tejanos maintained a semblance of influence in south Texas, in part by continuing a *patrón* system that directed the rank and file to "vote" for specific candidates and platforms. Anglo and Mexican bosses thus dominated communities for the rest of the century; but by the 1880s, these political standard-bearers faced opposition from competitors in the cities representing trends toward modernity. However, this political competition aimed at objectives other than uplifting the masses, for the new merchant class in the urban areas had in mind winning followers for their interests, thus disabling the Anglo and Mexican bosses. Montejano observes that the Tejano community generally met the challenge of post-

1850s politics by actively adapting traditional modes of participation in governance to the dominance of arriving Anglos.[3]

On a superficial level of analysis, the idea of passive political response that Cuellar posits appears to have some merit. For instance no Mexican American has been governor of Texas, and there is no record of a Tejano holding any other high-level administrative post in the nineteenth century.[4] Political offices occupied by Tejanos tended almost exclusively to be legislative posts, and even these were few in number and confined to areas in the Mexican settlement region. The first twenty-six legislatures, convened between 1846 and 1900, included over thirty-three hundred total members, with more than eight hundred in the state senate and twenty-five hundred in the House. Tejanos filled only two Senate positions; both held by the same man, José Antonio Navarro. In the state house, Mexican Americans took eleven seats, but only eight men occupied them.[5] Put another way, Tejanos filled less than one-half of 1 percent of all openings in the Texas legislature between 1846 and 1900. Nine of the thirteen total positions were filled by Mexican Americans in the early part of the period between 1846 and 1879. Only three Tejanos took elected seats in the house in the 1880s; only one in the 1890s.[6] Mexican-American incumbency on the state level was evidently not only sparse, but also waned in the latter decades of the century. Do these facts demonstrate that the transition of the era reflected negatively on Mexicanos, causing them to become politically submissive? Other lines of inquiry contest this.

A more complete analysis of Tejano officeholding and other forms of political participation indicates a flexible response by Texas Mexicans. Instead of capitulating to a new Anglo-controlled power structure, political activity among diverse groups within the Mexican settlement region manifested a variety of adaptive efforts aimed at creating and seizing opportunities to exercise influence.

In reality state and federal offices were not the only ones of potential political significance to an ethnic group of the nineteenth century. There were also county and city offices to be filled, and these may well have been more relevant to Tejanos than state or national positions. Alwyn Barr, in his account of post–Civil War political trends in Texas, has shown that issues of county and city government came to outweigh state or national ones for many, if not most Texans, after the early 1870s (during Conservative Reconstruction). According to Barr this situation initially resulted from the state administration's reactions against the tide of Radical Reconstruction. After Redemption the state moved to grant high degrees of autonomy to the governments of counties and cities, which, it should be noted, were multiplying rapidly at this time.[7] As a result county government evolved into and remained a highly significant policy-making unit up to as late as the 1930s. County officials commanded uncontested administrative authority over such matters as tax assessment and collection, administration of elections, and provision of social services. County governmental processes were quite void of any federal and state oversight or regulation until as late as 1931. Not until then, for example, did the state comptroller of public accounts demand that the counties submit annual records of revenues and expenditures. Even then the law lacked enforcement provisions.[8]

Given the extent of localized political networks, analyzing the degree of Tejano involvement at this level is difficult and complex. Little systematic evidence presently exists, but studies of local politics produced in the 1980s point to a need to depart from the model of nineteenth-century Mexican-American acquiescence. Inquiries such as those conducted by Arnoldo De León, Mario T. García, and David Montejano note that while factors such as age, naturalization status, and disenfranchisement deterred Tejanos from equal political participation, activism nevertheless took several forms.[9] For example Mexican-American leaders had consistent success in getting themselves elected or appointed to a variety of county and city offices in the last half of the nineteenth century. In San Antonio and Bexar County, for one, Tejanos held incumbencies in posts ranging from city council and county commission to collector, assessor, treasurer, and others. It is true that, as their numbers declined proportionately in the San Antonio and Bexar County population, their representation in local governmental offices also fell. Yet despite the decline, Tejanos took numerous offices of various types after 1865, and many held local government posts into the 1880s. In the closing decade of the nineteenth century, however, Tejano representation in elected or appointed offices within San Antonio and Bexar County came to an end, as the demography of the area played against their political ambitions.[10]

Documentation of an increasing, or at least consistent, Tejano presence in local political offices in areas where Mexicans had a numerical edge (e.g., in Laredo and Webb county, Brownsville and Cameron County, and El Paso and El Paso County) further weakens the case for Tejano passivity in the face of modernizing forces.[11] As Conservative Reconstruction promoted a shift of power from state and federal levels to local governmental units, Tejanos transferred their political energies appropriately. Furthermore their participation in the Mexican settlement region branched out from the holding of offices into other areas of politics, such as party activities. Through party politics Tejanos sought to convey their views of a range of issues of national as well as state and local significance. The various stands they took mirrored the complexity of the Mexican-American experience during this era. Thus Tejanos expressed divergent political views on the sectionalism of the 1850s, the meaning of the Civil War, on Reconstruction, and even on the issue of political bossism. In the 1870s, 1880s, and 1890s, Tejanos mustered campaigns to support presidential candidates, to aid community efforts to attract railroads, and to rally electoral support for state and local partisans deemed to represent Mexican-American interests.[12]

As did other aggrieved groups after midcentury, then, Tejanos used the available spectrum of political opportunities for expressing their political interests. Similarly Mexican-American leaders in nineteenth-century Texas, who generally descended from property-holding elements within the community, displayed a variety of political styles and strategies. Although definitive biographies of such noteworthy men as Juan N. Cortina, José Antonio Navarro, Santos Benavides, Catarino Garza, or Manuel Guerra are lacking, it is clear even from a cursory review of their lives and times that their political activities were responses to historical forces.

To be sure the story of Juan Cortina is dramatic testimony to violent Tejano resistance against the political and legal methods employed by Anglo Americans. Anglos had arrived in the lower Río Grande Valley following the Treaty of Guadalupe Hidalgo, where they established themselves in a society that was demographically and culturally Mexican. Indeed an international boundary separating Texas from Tamaulipas did not exist in the minds of most of the indigenous population, and Cortina in fact conducted business on both sides of the river. Despite their numerical inferiority and minority status in this ranching region, Anglos had nonetheless effectively expanded their hegemony by acquiring lands through a variety of mechanisms, among them accommodation and intermarriage with the daughters of local elites, but also by employing fraudulent means. Cortina's own experience with the newcomers had not been auspicious. He had seen portions of his family's landholdings reduced through Anglo-controlled court proceedings. In 1859 an open war broke out in Brownsville and along the border as Cortina and followers from both Texas and Mexico reacted against Anglo domination.[13]

Why Cortina took up arms in 1859, fought against the Confederacy, and continued attacking Anglo Texans until the mid-1870s remains a subject of debate. Some writers see him as a defender of Mexican rights, others as a brigand.[14] More recently one historian depicts him as a south Texas *caudillo* (regional strongman), arguing that Cortina's decision to champion the cause of the Mexican masses (while the elite was divided in its support for him) stemmed from personal frustration over thwarted desires for power, not from a sincere effort to help the Tejano people. Nonetheless efforts to attain political power for Mexican Americans were common along the border. Just as wealthy and powerful Anglos in south Texas used the judicial system to deprive Mexicans of their land, Cortina turned to violent action to protect his own rights.[15] Resistance in the style of Juan Cortina was one political option open to nineteenth-century Tejanos.

The careers of other Mexican-American political leaders prior to the Civil War do not show Cortina's will to resist. José Antonio Navarro, for example, can hardly be described as hostile to Anglo-American expansion in Texas. He is most aptly understood as an accommodating, middle-class politician in a geographic region readily distinguishable from Cortina's south Texas. By the time of annexation, Tejanos had become a minority in central Texas, and Navarro's hometown of San Antonio already had pretensions of emerging as a bustling center for goods departing westward. Born in 1795, Navarro formed friendships with Stephen F. Austin and other early Anglo settlers in 1821. Over the course of his political life, he served in such capacities as delegate to the constitutional conventions of 1836 and 1845, representative to the Third Congress of the Republic of Texas (1838–39), and senator in the First and Second Texas State legislatures (1846–49). On the one hand, Navarro's career was that of a man striving to transcend ethnic ties while advancing a vision of the Texas interest. In the 1820s, for example, he assisted vigorously in Anglo colonization projects and championed the cause of lending legal sanction to slavery in Texas. Toward the end of his life, the same impulse rang through his support of the secession movement in 1861 and of the Confederacy thereafter.[16] In the view of some historians, these aspects of Navarro's life have earned him the label, probably too often applied to accommodating minority politicians, of a Mexican "Uncle Tom."[17] But other aspects of his politics belie this image and show that he could not turn away completely from the specific interests of Tejanos. His almost single-handed defeat of a movement at the Convention of 1845 to disenfranchise Mexican voters is but one example testifying to this side of Navarro.[18]

The careers of Cortina and Navarro demonstrate that Tejano political leadership ranged from angry rejection of Anglo-American encroachment into the world of Tejanos to accommodation and even enthusiasm toward the promise of progress and prosperity. The postbellum years show a similar diversity of styles. On the one hand were Navarro-type accommodationists like Santos Benavides.[19] Scion of the original founders of Laredo, Benavides resided in a region where Anglos streaming into south Texas after the Mexican War had adjusted well. In that section of the borderland, the Anglo minority had formed coalitions with old landholders and merchants like Benavides. Benavides then went on to engage Cortina in 1859 and to serve as a Confederate officer on the battlefield. He participated in Laredo politics almost all his life, serving as the city's mayor in 1857 and 1858, and then as chief justice of Webb County. After terms as alderman in the city government following the Civil War, he left for the Texas House of Representatives, winning elections from 1879 through 1885. As a member of the legislature, he served on the House Committee on Public Health, the Committee on Agriculture and Stock Raising, the Insurance and Statistics Committee, and other bodies organized for the purpose of improving the state's general welfare. Like that of Navarro the theme of his political career was to transcend ethnic differences to advance the social and economic development of his home district, the border region. Also like Navarro, Benavides gained the respect of his Anglo Texas colleagues in the legislature by virtue of this political motif.[20]

By the 1880s Tejano politicians of the Navarro-Benavides persuasion lost their statewide prominence. The forces of modernization thawed the coalition that had existed between Anglos and Texas Mexican elites in the ranch society of the Mexican settlement region. The politics of transition after the 1880s fell to merchants and professionals in the towns, who judged the system of governance regressive. These new political competitors targeted the recruitment of Mexicans to dilute the voting strength of the old rural rulers. Tejano politicians participated in these local power struggles, but the poor remained outside the system. Such a situation gave impetus to the newspaper activist Catarino Garza, whose political protest spanned the period from the late 1880s to the early 1890s.[21]

Born in Matamoros and raised in the Brownsville area, Garza took an intense interest in the politics of Mexico and pledged himself to the overthrow of the dictator Porfirio Díaz. From the prevalently ranching counties of Starr and Duval, where Tejanos predominated, he issued strident criticisms against the government in

Mexico. He was equally sensitive to the discomforting conditions of lower-class Tejanos, many of whom had arrived in the 1880s because of severe conditions in Mexico under Díaz and because changing economic forces created a demand for more workers in south Texas. As he used his journalism to help organize mutual support in combating social discrimination, this middle-class Tejano amassed notoriety and admiration among the poor on both sides of the Río Grande for confronting conditions they perceived as oppressive.

When, in 1891, Garza led an abortive expedition against Díaz and retreated to Texas, ordinary people helped him elude the Texas Rangers and federal troops dispatched to capture him for violation of neutrality laws. For weeks he evaded the searchers and, in early 1892, covered by Tejano sympathizers, he made his way to the Texas coast and finally to Key West, Florida. There he helped Cuban exiles fight against the Spanish monarchy. Afterward he went on to Central America to fight for more liberal causes. His modus operandi was that of a nonpolitician, first using the press to air injustices and then becoming a guerrilla fighter when concessions did not follow. His activities during the latter years of his stay in Texas place him close to the mold of "social bandit."[22]

The career of Manuel Guerra points to still another type of political strategy practiced by nineteenth-century Tejanos. The descendent of settlers who had received land grants along the border in the 1760s, Guerra had learned the English language and American business techniques from a merchant in Corpus Christi. In the 1870s he settled in Roma to open a retail business and take control of the Guerra ranchlands in Starr County. In the mid-1880s he established his political base at Roma with the support of Jim Wells, Cameron County political boss. From 1894 until his death in 1915, Guerra served in the Starr County Commissioners' Court, ruling the county as the Demo-

cratic Party political strongman by warding off every reform challenge launched against bossism by newcomers
to the area. Safe within the confines of a ranching county
unattractive to merchants and farmers, the Guerra family
continued to dominate Starr County government into the
post–World War II era.[23]

Tejano leaders evidently modified their political approaches so as to deal with the slow but sure change
unfolding in the Mexican settlement region. Nevertheless
their political influence was ineffectual, and Mexicanos
remained a disadvantaged collectivity. An explanation
for Mexican-American inability to make the body politic
receptive to community needs is therefore in order.

Three elements played key roles in restricting Tejano
participation in Texas politics during the era of change.
First the Tejanos' Spanish-Mexican heritage produced a
lingering influence that inclined them to perceive community leaders as inherently acting on behalf of the people,
and this association almost certainly compromised their
potential for effective political action. Second, Anglo
Americans, thinking themselves superior to Mexicans,
refused them a full partnership in the politics of the state.
Third, certain demographic forces served to the advantage of Anglos and diluted the voice of the Tejanos at the
voting polls.

Aspects of culture certainly affected the ways in which
Tejanos and Anglos approached the achievement of political goals in Texas. In the case of Tejanos living in the
Mexican settlement region, a good many were born in
Mexico with only recently broken ties to the Spanish institutions of their mother country. The sense of trust and
loyalty that members of that tradition attached to political
and social superordinates likely influenced the political
behavior of a major segment of Mexicans holding the
voting franchise. Primary documents of the nineteenth

century allude to many incidents of Mexicans voting as indicated by white leaders.

Much of the historical literature on this matter holds that there was a system of peonage, a lingering residue of the old Spanish-Mexican feudal system in which peasants surrendered their political voice to the patrón, or boss, in exchange for basic sustenance. The picture is one of a relationship of subservience on the part of the peon and paternalism on behalf of the patrón. This agreement, scholars have long argued, served as the cornerstone of "bossism" in Texas politics. The historian Evan Anders, for example, contends that:

> The Mexican American constituents [of the Jim Wells machine] were receptive to Wells' gestures of friendship and support. Lacking any tradition of participation in electoral politics, they did not view themselves as independent voters or as an aggrieved interest group with the potential power to organize and force their demands on public officials. Instead, the heritage of peonage conditioned the Hispanic workers and farmers to define their political role in terms of personal obligation . . . The reciprocity of the old feudal system survived.[24]

That participation in machine politics was characteristic of Mexican Americans, especially in south Texas and the El Paso Valley, hardly seems refutable. Additionally the idea that Tejanos did not see themselves as an aggrieved interest group striving to force political leaders into advancing their individual and ethnic demands seems plausible at first glance.

However, the understanding that Tejano loyalty to the leaders of political machines was a survival of feudalism rests on shaky ground. First there exists an ambiguity in the language of this view. Anders's analysis asserts that "The reciprocity of the old feudal system survived." Does this mean that machine politics in south Texas operated through the actual structure of a feudality? Can it be assumed that empirically accessible norms and codes were in place in that society that cast peasants in the status of "peons" and imposed the implied fealty and obligation?

The claim that a feudal system identified the areas where bossism existed must be questioned because there is a paucity of primary evidence to support the contention. If, on the other hand, the contention is that feudalism formed a legacy of the culture of Mexico that shaped the mentality of Tejano peasants to choose peonage over active participation in politics, then again the argument is totally void of primary ethnographic documentation. The proposition that a feudal political structure was extant in Texas, or that peasants viewed themselves as peons and retreated into political submission of their own accord rests on scant evidence. All that can be said factually is that Tejanos did show loyalty to political leaders, some of whom used their allegiance as the basis for assembling political machines.

That bossism was quite common in the United States during the era under study suggests that this form of politics was an outgrowth of a failure to deliver on the promise of democracy. Disadvantaged groups everywhere turned to the system to receive benefits that could not be secured otherwise. Thus to say without supporting documentation that the Texas machines flourished because of the survival of Mexican feudalism is, to borrow a phrase from William Ryan, a case of "blaming the victim." [25]

Another empirical flaw of traditional historical explanations regarding Tejano roles in politics is the assumption that Mexicans where unfamiliar with certain democratic traditions. This, quite frankly, is a distortion of history. Not only is evidence to support this point lacking, but there is documentation to the contrary. As social historians make clear, the involvement of citizens in political matters related to community administration was evident in the days of colonial Texas.[26] Moreover people of Mexican origin pursued varying political strategies and styles after 1836. The Tejano political heritage may have rested on a system of values somewhat divergent from the electoral system of late-nineteenth-century Texas and the United States, but Texas Mexicans did not lack experience with democracy.

The shortcomings in the interpretation that political bossism grew out of the survival of feudal peonage are most deceptive because a close reading of the philosophical nature of the Tejano political heritage makes evident an alternate plausible understanding of Mexican-American loyalty to the nineteenth-century bosses. A central tenet in the Mexican governmental and legal tradition is its elevation of community and state interests over those of the individual.[27] This aspect of political culture stemmed most probably from the link between the Roman and Spanish traditions of law and governance, rather than from any legacy of feudalism. Given that the mass of Tejanos identified with an ethos more strongly inclined toward the perception of power as a means to adjudicate claims of competing groups, or as a resource for advancing an abstract collective interest, it would seem only natural that they felt loyalty to political leaders (or ranch *patrones*) as guardians of the community. What may have seemed to the Anglo mind an illogical allegiance rooted in indolence could well have been an expression of a greater communal interest, based on the descent of the legal and governmental traditions of Tejanos. Indeed, many of the nation's immigrants during this period, most of whom came with the political heritage of the southern and eastern portions of Europe, clung to similar traditions, much to the perplexity of social reformers and other native-born Americans of the age. While some elements of the Tejano community saw bossism as a way of participating in the system, others just as clearly pursued other means.

Such contrasting political behavior was in keeping with the diversity of the Tejano heritage.

Although Mexican culture contributed, in an ironic way, to the subordinate status of Mexican Americans in Texas politics, more forceful in weakening Tejano power was the ethic of the Anglo-American majority. In contradistinction to the Mexican tradition, the Anglo experience stressed individualistic values. This orientation, as Alexis de Toqueville noticed in his early travels to America, posed both a threat to democratic order, in the form of a tendency toward tyranny of the majority, and a solution, in the form of a proclivity for the formation of political associations and interest groups.[28] Again it is plausible that this particular approach to democracy, though not democracy per se, seemed foreign to the mass of Tejanos. More important is that whites, who saw the political process in such individualistic and oppositional terms, probably considered Mexicans to be foreign to the system.

The degree of difference Anglos perceived between themselves and the Spanish-speaking population in the Mexican settlement region contributed adversely to the political condition of Tejanos. In their most extreme form, white perceptions translated racism into politics. The earliest of white settlers, Arnoldo De León shows in his detailed survey of nineteenth-century writings, manifested a "color consciousness" that led to perceptions of Tejanos as a mongrel, half-breed people resembling other minorities disenfranchised by law and tradition. Anglos further pictured Mexicans as morally defective, irresponsibly indolent, and only questionably American.[29]

Such racist and xenophobic attitudes worked to provide not only a justification for Anglo domination in Texas, but also an explanation for the exclusion and subordination of Tejanos in the political process. It was on the basis of such ideas that rebellious Mexican activists such as Cortina and Garza, whose appeal was transnational, could be portrayed as enemies of civility, then ostracized. On the same basis Mexican voters (both native- and foreign-born) participating in machine politics could be pictured as ignorant, uncaring, feudalistic peons, incapable of exercising a full measure of civic responsibility and deserving of exclusion from full political participation. In such a milieu, only the accommodating Tejano elites (such as Navarro, Benavides, and Guerra) could be afforded political legitimacy by the white community. Others in the spectrum, Tejano activists and the masses alike, deserved less.

Another set of forces contributing to the disadvantaged status of Tejanos in politics was demographic in nature. Demographic trends in the Mexican settlement region severely diluted any possibility of building a coalition of Mexican voters that could have rivaled Anglos at election time. Even if Tejanos had been inclined more uniformly to organize as an aggrieved interest group, demography would have denied success at any level above the isolated local areas, mainly along the Río Grande, where they did at times exercise dominant political influence.

The first demographic effect denied the Tejanos majority standing in the population as a whole; contrary to widespread popular impression, Mexicans did not comprise a majority of the population in the south, central, and western portions of the state after midcentury (see table 8). In 1850 they formed a narrow majority of 50.1 percent in these areas combined, but in subsequent decades their presence declined to about 40 percent. Tejanos thus could not build political strength at the regional level based on numerical majority in the population as a whole. They composed only a minority of the potential constituents, and while they were a sizable minority, Anglos outnumbered them after 1850.

Further diluting their political potential were the sex

Table 8   Ethnic Composition of Eligible Voting Population, Mexican Settlement Region, 1850–1900

Estimates	Mexican Region				
	1850	1860	1870	1880	1900
Population of Sample Counties	20,859	45,714	75,153	139,982	390,108
Percent Males 21 Years and Over	30.5%	28.2%	27.1%	26.6%	24.8%
Number of Eligible Voters	6,361	12,888	20,398	37,185	57,682
	Tejanos Only				
Population of Sample Counties	10,458	17,745	27,972	53,513	127,335
Percent Males 21 Years and Over	25.0%	26.1%	25.9%	26.3%	24.1%
Number of Eligible Voters	2,617	4,626	7,256	14,046	19,416
	Anglos Only				
Population of Sample Counties	9,109	25,463	32,439	62,788	130,833
Percent Males 21 Years and Over	34.8%	29.8%	29.1%	26.7%	25.7%
Number of Eligible Voters	3,173	7,585	9,454	16,734	31,102

Note: Estimated population sizes are based on reports of the Census Bureau, *U.S. Census of Population,* 1850.1, pp. xcv–cii; 1860.0, pp. 282–85; 1870.1, pp. 63–64; 1880.1, pp. 78–81; and 1900.1, pp. 40–42. All other estimates in the table are derived from the sample data and any discrepancies are due to rounding errors in the percentages. The sample sizes were as follows: (1) 5,380 for 1850; (2) 11,374 for 1860; (3) 17,824 for 1870; (4) 25,945 for 1880; and (5) 40,768 for 1900. It should be noted that the percentages in Table 8 are not the percent of eligible voters. The estimated number of eligible voters for the decades 1850–80 includes all males twenty-one years old or over. Because voting laws changed in the mid-1890s, the 1900 estimates of eligible voters include all native-born males twenty-one years old or over, plus those of foreign birth who were naturalized or had filed intention papers. Voting-age males listed in the census as "aliens" were excluded from the estimates for 1900. All estimates in the table are adjusted to account for variations in sampling fractions (see Preface).

and age characteristics of the Tejano population. There were a greater number of females among Mexicans than among Anglos, and the Tejanos were a younger people than were the whites in the region. Since females and young people (those below twenty-one years of age) did not share in the franchise, a smaller proportion of Mexicans was eligible to vote. According to estimates of eligible voting populations, Anglo voters outnumbered Tejano voters in the region by ratios of 1.2 to 1 in 1850, 1.6 to 1 in 1860, 1.3 to 1 in 1870, 1.2 to 1 in 1880, and 1.6 to 1 in 1900 (see table 8). This was the case even though the Tejanos comprised a majority of the Mexican settlement region's population in 1850, and even though Anglos outnumbered Tejanos only by ratios of 1.4 to 1 in 1860, 1.3 to 1 in 1870 and 1880, and 1.1 to 1 in 1900.

The immigration and naturalization status of the Tejanos also worked against their participation in politics. By 1900 the naturalization of foreign-born residents affected eligibility for voting because of a change in state election laws during the mid-1890s. After that time only those immigrants who were naturalized or who filed intention papers could vote, and this reduced the opportunity for Tejano participation by an added degree. The sample data from twenty counties in the Mexican region show this clearly. Two-thirds of Tejano males over twenty years old in 1900 were foreign-born, and of these only 46.1 percent had been naturalized or had filed intention papers. The net result was that about 36 percent of male Mexicanos over twenty could not participate in the franchise because of their "alien" status under the new election code. The reduction of voter eligibility among Anglos was far less severe. Only 23.4 percent of white males over twenty years of age were foreign-born, and about 69 percent of them had been naturalized or had filed intention papers in 1900. Where the legal change excluded some 36 percent of Tejano males over twenty, it barred only about 7 percent of Anglo males from participation.

Although it is difficult to assess the effects of other demographic traits on political participation in any exact terms, a profile of the Tejano and Anglo voting populations suggests further impacts on Mexican-American political participation (see table 9). If political activity was related to socioeconomic status, as many twentieth-century studies have shown, then the Tejanos' social position may have operated to depress their participation. Anglo males who were eligible to vote were more likely involved in occupations within the specialized sectors of the economy, while potential Tejano voters more frequently worked in unspecialized labor roles. Indeed by 1900 about 79 percent of white voters in the Mexican region engaged in agriculture, personal and professional service, trade and transportation, or manufacturing and mechanical occupations. Only 42.3 percent of the Mexicanos worked in these fields, while half had unspecialized jobs. Anglo voters, in other words, were engaged in occupations that may have given them a larger vested interest in the political process, while the Tejanos' economic standing could have been an alienating factor. Considering further that Anglos in the voting population were both more wealthy and more likely to be literate, they may well have had more resources with which to secure and conserve their political interests. In short the socioeconomic characteristics of the eligible Mexican voters in the nineteenth century suggest a group susceptible to political nonparticipation.

Several factors accompanying the shifts of nineteenth-century Texas affected Tejano approaches to political participation. Lack of resources and exclusion from specialized-labor markets impaired their pursuit of political interests, the demography of the Mexican settlement region diluted their collective political voice, disdain on

Table 9   Profile of Tejano and Anglo Voting Populations,
Mexican Settlement Region, 1850–1900

	1850	1860	1870	1880	1900
	Tejanos				
Occupational Classification					
Agriculture	20.0%	28.9%	21.3%	29.4%	22.0%
Personal and Professional					
Service	0.3%	8.6%	4.8%	7.6%	6.1%
Trade and Transportation	9.1%	8.1%	6.8%	6.5%	7.8%
Manufacturing and					
Mechanical	10.1%	8.7%	6.1%	6.6%	6.4%
Unspecialized	0.2%	36.6%	53.7%	43.4%	50.0%
Wealth Holders	13.6%	41.5%	16.3%	—	—
Less than $501	5.0%	32.9%	12.4%	—	—
$501–$1000	2.7%	4.0%	1.8%	—	—
$1001–$5000	4.6%	3.7%	1.8%	—	—
Over $5000	1.3%	0.9%	0.4%	—	—
Literate	27.5%	36.3%	26.2%	33.0%	20.3%
Sample Size	690	1215	1882	3096	3976
	Anglos				
Occupational Classification					
Agriculture	15.3%	33.3%	33.0%	41.7%	34.9%
Personal and Professional					
Service	25.8%	18.0%	21.6%	14.5%	12.1%
Trade and Transportation	14.2%	18.4%	13.8%	15.9%	19.9%
Manufacturing and					
Mechanical	15.9%	13.9%	14.1%	10.7%	12.0%
Unspecialized	—	7.8%	8.3%	10.9%	10.8%
Wealth Holders	33.5%	51.5%	38.3%	—	—
Less than $501	11.6%	21.9%	20.0%	—	—
$501–$1000	5.7%	6.7%	6.9%	—	—
$1001–$5000	11.5%	14.0%	9.2%	—	—
Over $5000	4.8%	8.9%	2.2%	—	—
Literate	95.5%	93.8%	92.8%	91.6%	91.9%
Sample Size	803	1871	2207	2820	4071

Note: All males twenty-one years old or over are included in the estimates for 1850–80. The 1900 estimates are based on males twenty-one years old or over who were native-born, naturalized, or who had filed for naturalization. All estimates in the table are adjusted to account for variations in sampling fractions (see Preface).

the part of white political culture muffled their ambitions, and their own political heritage inclined them toward democratic values that diverged somewhat from those of Anglos. Such forces had unnerving influences, and some segments within the constituency yielded to them. Still others thought the politics of the age confusing and were ill-prepared to deal with them. Alternatively, however, concerned members from the successful elite and from the masses as well faced up to the challenges and coped with them. Tejanos of diverse backgrounds maintained a varied interest in the politics of Texas and struggled to make their political interests known and their influence felt. Still, as in the economic fold, the transition to modernity in politics was Anglo dominated. The new politics amplified the voices of whites and diminished that of Mexicanos.

Structural Development, Education, and Literacy

T he modernization of society everywhere involves the development of formal schooling systems; the transformation of Texas from frontier to modernity in the late nineteenth century is no exception.[1] The years between 1850 and 1900 frame the period in which the basic building blocks of the Texas system of education emerged. Indeed as one analysis of the history of public schooling in Texas indicates, the period between 1860 and 1884 quite precisely marks the watershed years when popular opposition to free public education changed to support of the idea among most Texans.[2]

Before looking at the connection between these new supportive views and the structural development of education in Texas, it is useful to recognize some aspects of the historical affinity between schooling and modernization. Here it is best to avoid the question of causal connections. The long-standing debate in the educational and sociological literatures over whether a formal educational system is a necessary condition for successful modernization is irrelevant to our analysis.[3] Of greater salience is the effort to comprehend, at least in outline form, the functional associations between organized school systems and the modernization process.

Political and economic modernization processes use school systems in a number of ways. Among the most widely recognized is the nation-building and work-force–development function of formal education. Since the origin of the public-schooling movement, political, educational, and business leaders in the United States have perceived the importance of this function of education in the making of modern society, and it is the subject of a great deal of scholarship dealing with learning institutions.[4] A less-obvious way that schools further the processes of modernization is by what may be termed their "problem-management" function. Historically dominant social groups have used formal schooling as an instrument to help avert challenges and hindrances to the social order presented by laborers, minorities, and the lower social classes. Through this function, education has become one of the primary mechanisms for managing "social problems."[5]

There is no systematic study of these connections in the case of the evolution of the Texas schools during the nineteenth century, but such relations are evident in the general history of the period.[6] For example many authors note the significance of educational issues in the Texas war for independence. In protest documents coming out of the conventions of the early 1830s and the Declaration of Independence in 1836, Anglo colonizers complained about the undeveloped state of education. Since the subsequent constitution and first congresses of the republic made little provision for the development of a school system, there is considerable debate over the sincerity and validity of Anglo Texan complaints.[7] Nevertheless Texan grievances that the Mexican government had failed to provide a means of support for schooling, to mandate the teaching of English in schools, and to allow a place for Protestant religious activities testify to a recognition of the utility of formal education in molding a sense of identification among the population. Whatever obstacles stood in the way of developing a system of schooling in those colonial and revolutionary days, and there were many, Anglo Texans clearly pursued a course that would lead eventually to the teaching of their language and not that of the Mexicans; to indoctrination in their religious values and not those of Tejanos; to the inculcation of their national heritage and not that of the Mexican Americans.[8] Two cultures were in contention, and the Anglos intended that theirs would dominate in the schools.[9]

Other elements of the historical chronology of Texas education point to the use of formal schooling to manage social problems in the transition toward modernity. The activities of the Peabody Fund in Texas and other southern states document efforts on the part of social leaders, both on the state and national levels, to institute a schooling process for dealing with problems posed by the free black population after the Civil War.[10] Recurrent nineteenth-century public debate over the benefits of providing free public education to the poor reveals a proclivity to use education as a mechanism for managing social problems.[11] In Texas as elsewhere in the world of the last century, the exigencies of change helped shape the evolution of the schooling system.

In the structure of the schooling process, the most dramatic change was expansion of the system. According to Census Bureau reports, more than 515,000 students attended Texas schools at the turn of the century, and the percentage of the school-aged population going to school increased from about 23 percent in 1850 to 42 percent in 1900.[12] A school-adequacy survey published by the Texas State Board of Education in 1937 shows that annual public expenditures increased eightfold between the 1871–72 and the 1899–1900 school years, reaching over $5 million in the latter year. This escalation in gross expenditures more than doubled the amount spent per pupil (from $1.81 to $4.25) and supported a rapid expansion in the number of independent school districts.[13] The expanded formal school system did not reach all members of Texas society equally however. Inequalities emerged along two dimensions. By the end of the nineteenth century, substantial regional disparities had evolved in provisions for schooling, and ethnic discrepancies within regions emerged as well.[14]

At the regional level, the spread of formal education followed a pattern matching that of the advancing Texas economy. As the conversion to a commercial and industrial system took root first in the Anglo settlement regions, coming only later to the Mexican sections, so it was with education. Using the officially defined "scholastic population" for comparison, the twenty counties in the Mexican settlement region covered in this study contained an estimated 9 percent of the state's scholastic-aged children in 1900.[15] The same counties accounted for only 5.6 percent of the statewide enrollment that year. Twenty years earlier, in 1880, the situation was much the same.[16] The school-attendance rate was significantly lower in the Mexican region compared to other sections of the state. Indeed where the 1937 school-adequacy survey estimates that 81.9 percent of the statewide scholastic population was enrolled in schools at the turn of the century, our calculations show that only 51.1 percent attended school in south, central, and west Texas.[17] The same figures for 1880 were 82.5 percent and 37.7 percent, respectively.[18] The general availability of modern formal schooling came later to the Mexican settlement region than to the decidedly Anglo areas of the state.

The same correspondence between schooling and economic change is evident at the sectional level within the Mexican settlement region.[19] In 1870, for example, about 36 percent of the scholastic-aged children attended school in the region's most advanced area of central Texas. The attendance rates in the south and west were 15 percent and 7 percent, respectively. Schooling came first to the most advanced areas, and only later to the fringes of the transition toward modernization.

Within the Mexican settlement region, ethnic inequalities in schooling also emerged. For example in south Texas at the turn of the century, Mexican-American children made up 88 percent of the scholastic-aged population. At the same time, they comprised only 79 percent of the children in school, and their rate of school attendance was only 31 percent.[20] Anglo children comprised only 10 percent of the relevant population, but they accounted for 19 percent of school pupils, and attended school at a rate of 66 percent. Similar disparities held in the central and west areas as well.[21] Overall Tejanos comprised 45 percent of the scholastic-aged children in the Mexican settlement region as a whole, but only 26 percent of those in school. Their rate of attendance was 29 percent, compared to 71 percent for Anglos, who accounted for only 44 percent of the scholastic-aged group in the region. As the educational system developed in Texas, it came late to the Mexican settlement region and later still to the Mexicans of that region.[22]

Inequities in the growth of education meant lost opportunity for developing the basic personal skills that modernizing nineteenth-century Texas certainly valued. An analysis of literacy rates among adults, for example, shows that this fundamental skill was lacking in the regional population, especially among Tejanos.[23] According to the Census Bureau, the statewide rate of literacy for adults twenty years of age and over did not increase between 1850 and 1900. In 1850 some 84.5 percent of Texas adults were literate, compared to 83.0 percent in 1900.[24] In contrast literacy rates for the Mexican settlement region in the same years were 60.1 percent and 71.6 percent, respectively. Despite gains in reading and writing abilities, the region's adult population lagged behind the relatively constant level of literacy for the state as a whole. As education came late to the Mexican settlement region, so did the fundamental skills it imparts.

What accounted for most of the literacy gap between the Mexican settlement region and the state was the exceedingly high level of illiteracy that existed within the Tejano community. Indeed illiterate Mexicanos comprised an estimated one-third or more of all illiterate adults in the state in 1850, and more than 14 percent in 1900.[25] The literacy rate among Tejanos at midcentury was only 25.7 percent. By 1900 this had increased to 39.3 percent, still appallingly low when compared to all of the state's adult population.[26]

Several plausible factors may explain such differences. Educational opportunities hardly existed in Mexico during the era of the late nineteenth century, so that those joining the migratory currents to Texas lacked literacy. Given the employment opportunities available to immigrants in Texas, moreover, the benefits of education may not have made much sense, at least to the first generation of adults. More relevant, however, was the impact of inequality in the development of Texas schools, a point documented by statistics on literacy in the various sections of the Mexican settlement region. In 1850 levels of adult Tejano literacy in each section stood at about 25 percent. By 1900, however, the region's most advanced section, central Texas, had a Tejano literacy rate of 42.4 percent, compared to levels of 38.5 percent and 36.2 percent in the lesser developed areas of south and west Texas, respectively.[27]

The late coming of schools to the Mexican settlement region hindered both the human resources needed for advancement and the opportunities open to residents for benefiting from the transformation of Texas economy and society. The region as a whole suffered from a lack of skill development, not only in its adult population as a whole, but also in its labor force. By 1900 for example, about 28 percent of adults who were pursuing gainful employment in the region were illiterate. Fifty years earlier, that proportion had been 22 percent. The lack of schooling actually resulted in a situation where the adult labor force had less skill at reading and writing at the turn of the century than had been the case in the earlier era of the frontier. Sectional comparisons, moreover, demonstrate the magnitude this trend reached in some locales. In south Texas, for instance, where both economic and educational growth lagged, the level of illiteracy in the adult labor force was 30 percent in 1850; this increased to 47 percent by 1900. In the more-developed section of central Texas, the labor-force illiteracy level of 17 percent for 1850 declined to 14 percent by 1900.[28] In the Mexican settlement region, and particularly its outlying areas, lagging economic advancement meant less educational service. Less education meant a less-skilled labor force, and a less-skilled labor force meant less opportunity for upward mobility.

This cycle of sagging economy and education was, no doubt, a formidable obstacle to the members of the Tejano community as they pursued their interests and well-being.

In fact by 1900 over half (53 percent) of the region's Mexican-American workers were illiterate, compared to an illiteracy rate among Anglo workers of just 1.6 percent. This difference, of course, meant that regional labor markets often pitted illiterate Mexicans against literate whites in competition for jobs, and the result is obvious from the deteriorating occupational standing of obreros.

Nevertheless a fact of central importance shown by the relation between literacy and occupational standing is that reading and writing skills counted very little for Tejanos. Data from 1900, for instance, show that 56.6 percent of literate adult Tejano workers secured jobs in the specialized production areas of agriculture, the services, trade, transportation, and manufacturing or mechanical vocations. The other 43.4 percent worked at unspecialized jobs. Among literate Anglo workers, in contrast, 88.7 percent found employment in the specialized trades, while only 11.3 percent fell into the unspecialized labor pool.

That the majority of illiterate Tejanos could find only unspecialized employments indicates that reading and writing ability did lead to a slight improvement in Mexican Americans' chances for better jobs. But simply being "Mexican" proved a stronger obstacle. The philosophy of the period deemphasized education for Mexicans. Anglo society, including many of its educators, looked upon Mexican people as suited only for laboring in the lowest occupations.[29] Such anti-Mexican sentiment blocked Tejanos from the pursuit of education for occupational gain, and quite likely put a drag on any commitment to the advancement of schooling in the region as a whole. For Tejanos, at any rate, education and its resulting skills had less payoff in the labor markets.

Perhaps a more significant way in which the inequalities of education worked to the detriment of Tejanos and their community has to do with the levels of adult female illiteracy that resulted. The lack of school development had a much more deleterious effect on the literacy of Mexicanas than on any other segment of the population. In 1850 the literacy rate of 27.4 percent for Mexican-American females matched that of Tejano males. But over the following fifty years, as the school system emerged, male Tejano literacy climbed nearly twenty points, to 46.2 percent; among Tejanas the rate increased only two points, to 29.6 percent. Mexican-American females, as a group, were among the most illiterate people in the Texas population by the turn of the century.

The significance of this exceedingly low level of literacy for Tejanas, of course, was not in its direct relation to chances for Mexican-American improvement in labor competition. Mexicanas, like other women of their time, were not often active in the labor force.[30] Yet as Elise Boulding has shown convincingly, women played key roles, little recognized, in historical modernization processes.[31] Their contribution related more to the welfare and betterment of their communities than to direct economic production. It was women, after all, who often energized the mutual-aid societies and welfare services that have since merged into the welfare state, and Boulding has made it clear that this contribution was especially crucial for various ethnic enclaves as they integrated and assimilated into the stream of American society.[32] The rise of education and the promotion of literacy, in other words, served to mitigate substantially the social problems of transformation and change, by imparting skills to women that enabled them to act as the backbone of community self-help and self-sustenance networks. In the Tejano community of the Mexican settlement region, however, neglect of education, inequalities in schooling, and excessive illiteracy in the female segment of the Mexican-American population hampered this development.[33]

Despite the hardships that inadequacies in school

advancement wrought for Tejanos, their desire and will to strive for better conditions remained undaunted. In particular there are two lines of historical investigation that indicate the resilience of Tejanos as they faced the struggle against the illiteracy of their people and for the advancement of their community. The first of these involves further statistical analysis of Mexican-American patterns of schooling in the nineteenth century. The second deals with such mutual-aid services as were available to Tejanos.

The main statistical information documenting the unrelenting desire of Mexicans to procure the means to better living conditions for themselves and their children concerns trends of school enrollment between 1850 and 1900. Over this time the general pattern of attendance among Tejanos of scholastic age was one of decline in the twenty years from 1850 to 1870, followed by a resurgence in the thirty years after 1870. Specifically the rate of attendance in 1850 was 23.5 percent. This fell by ten points to 13.3 percent in 1870, then rose to 29 percent by 1900. The children of immigrant Mexicans, moreover, accounted for much of the increase in the latter period.[34]

The important thing to notice about this pattern is not the small magnitude of Tejano attendance rates in the nineteenth century, since they are explained by the inadequacies of educational development in Texas as discussed above. Rather it is the responsiveness of the rates to social conditions defining educational opportunities for Tejanos that is significant. The period of declining attendance between 1850 and 1870 corresponds to times when Mexicans were militarily, then economically and politically, subjugated to the hegemony of the United States and Anglo Texan institutions. Anti-Mexican sentiment among whites, volatile and sometimes violent resistance among Mexicans, and the rigors of civil war made this an era for allowing the education of Mexicans to deteriorate;

even for dismantling and disrupting what opportunities remained. Indeed the fact that school attendance rates for whites of scholastic age declined from 42.6 percent in 1850 to 40.5 percent in 1870 shows that this was not even a period of advancing education for Anglos in the region, let alone for the Tejanos. Given the conditions of the time, diminishing rates of school attendance among Mexicans are not surprising.

In the latter·thirty years of the century, however, conditions were different. Though anti-Mexican attitudes remained, this was a period of optimism and expanding horizons in Texas; a time of general economic growth and political reform. The winds of change in white society made it a time for advancing education, and the fact that school reforms through the years finally succeeded in establishing the foundations of what was to become the public system of education is indication enough. These currents, combined with the determination of Tejanos to assert their interests, correspond to the escalation of school attendance. Mexican participation in schools, then, responded to opportunity. When chances to get an education were reduced, Tejano participation dwindled. When greater opportunity was present, participation moved ahead.

Also indicating of their determination to assert the interest of their community in the field of education was the degree to which mutual-aid activity among Tejanos focused on concerns about schooling. Indeed as José Amaro Hernández in his account of Chicano mutual-aid makes clear, the latter years of the nineteenth century were flourishing times for Mexican-American fraternal and benevolent societies. Such organizations as the Sociedad Mutualista Benito Juárez, the Sociedad Mutualista Miguel Hidalgo, and the Sociedad Ignacio Zaragoza, along with numerous others were formed during this era in a movement to bond together Mexican Americans in mutual defense of the community and to provide for acute need.[35]

Mutual-aid organizations in the Tejano community provided a variety of services, such as burial assistance and aid to survivors, legal advising, social and recreational gatherings, care of the sick, and welfare to the needy. Not least among their goals, however, was a concerted effort to promote the education of Mexican Americans by such means as holding benefits for schools; establishing museums, libraries, and publications; and in some cases founding their own learning institutions. Their prevailing philosophy, according to Hernández, was to break down the inequities of schools for Mexicans and to urge the proper preparation of their youth for participation in the mainstream of American life.[36] Even though the skills imparted by education held little promise of reward for Tejanos in their struggle for economic and financial betterment, they never gave up their belief in schooling. In this they were resilient and steadfast.

As the state moved to develop a public education system in the late nineteenth century, school administrators neglected Tejanos. Similar to economic and political modernization, educational services in the Mexican region lagged behind other parts of the state. Provisions for schooling in the outlying south- and west-Texas regions trailed developments in more advanced central Texas, and when schools were established in the Mexican region, they served Anglo children foremost. The modernization of education, therefore, did more to improve skills and open opportunity for whites. It left Tejanos further behind.

Households
and
Families

Composition,
Convergence, and
Cultural Perceptions

D emographic, economic, political, and educational variables account in part for imbalances between Anglos and Mexicans during the nineteenth century, but the structural features of Texas society were not the only things that changed. This chapter focuses on Anglo attitudes toward Tejanos as another factor. Specifically the views whites held about Mexican family life provide an arena to describe how attitudes helped make Texas into a society with not room enough for Mexican Americans.

Often scholarly analyses take

for granted the assumption that prejudice is at the root of inequalities between minority and dominant groups. In recent years a debate has surfaced about reassessing this notion. Social-science literature observes that organized efforts to bring minority and dominant group members into contact with one another, such as school desegregation programs, often do not result in the relaxation of prejudice. In exploring the reasons why simply "getting people together" does not always moderate feelings of alienation, sociologists have found that the reduction of prejudice requires more than contact between peoples. It also seems to demand that parties make contact with equal standing in situations calling for cooperative action toward mutual goals. A clear implication of this sociological finding is that prejudice and inequality breed upon one another in competitive and conflicting social relations.[1]

To explore what role attitudes played in the social inequities that emerged between Tejanos and Anglos, we first explore the structure and composition of Anglo and Mexican households and the adjustments each made as Texas underwent the transition to modernization. Then we turn directly to questions concerning the role of ethnocentrism and prejudice in the social history of relations between Texas Mexicans and Anglos. Were the Anglos of Texas prejudiced from the beginning of their encounters with Tejanos, and was their prejudice a source of tension and inequality? Alternatively, did feelings of alienation between Tejanos and whites arise as rationalizations for inequalities that emerged during a time of competition, conflict, and struggle? Precisely how did the drive toward modernity reflect on attitudes Anglos held about Tejanos, particularly about their family patterns?

An investigation of household and family life among Tejanos presents an opportunity to assess these questions, because living arrangements serve as central forces in transmitting cultural traditions and shaping individual

Table 10   Tejano and Anglo Household Types,
1850 and 1900

Household Types	Tejanos		Anglos	
	1850	1900	1850	1900
Nuclear	81.5%	74.1%	73.5%	73.8%
Extended	16.5%	18.4%	16.8%	16.9%
Single Person	1.7%	7.0%	6.4%	7.9%
Undetermined	0.3%	0.5%	3.3%	1.4%
Sample Size	594	4555	456	3406

Note: The sample sizes represent the number of households incorporated into the sample data from south, central, and west Texas in 1850 and 1900.

personalities. Consequently many persistent expressions of alienation between minority and dominant groups have involved images of households and families. Current popular ideology, for instance, regards the Mexican-American household and family as inflexible in its ties to custom and tradition.[2]

What the data from the federal censuses of the nineteenth century show is that during the transition occurring in the last decades of the century, household types adapted to the structural changes in the different regions of Texas.[3] This was true, moreover, for both Mexicans and Anglos (see table 10). The variations provide elementary evidence of the responses Mexican Americans and Anglos made to structural changes in the wider society.

In 1850 the proportion of households occupied by nuclear families among Tejanos was higher than for whites by about seven percentage points. The number of single-person households in the Anglo community surpassed the number for Tejanos by nearly 5 percent. Extended-family households comprised near equal percentages in each group.[4] By the turn of the century, the situation had changed. Among Tejanos the proportion of nuclear-family households had declined from 81.5 percent to 74.1 percent, bringing the number of these household types in the Tejano community more into line with their presence among Anglos. In the same period, the percentage of extended-family households among Mexicans increased from 16.5 to 18.4 percent, and single-person households grew from 1.7 to 7.0 percent.[5]

Changes in the household composition of Tejanos in the nineteenth century raise several questions. Why did the proportion of Mexicans living in single-person households increase to a level approaching the practice of this living arrangement among Anglos? Why did the pattern of Tejano household composition become more similar to that of whites between 1850 and 1900? Why did the composition of Tejano households change significantly at all? In this area, as in many others discussed before, it appears that there was a process of adaptation to historical change.

In explicitly asking why patterns of Mexican and Anglo living arrangements converged toward similarity between 1850 and 1900, only a few logical possibilities present themselves. One possibility is that through exposure to Anglo Americans, the Mexicans of Texas learned and accepted the way of life of whites. However, the competitive, often hostile, relations between Mexican and Anglo Texans would seem to preclude an explanation based on a process of mass acculturation or assimilation. Another possibility is that both Anglos and Mexicans in nineteenth-century Texas encountered similar living conditions; circumstances influenced each group to adjust its household composition patterns in a similar way. Indeed this kind of explanation, positing that historical change created a convergence of Mexican and Anglo living arrangements, is not only consistent with the aggregate data given in table 10, but is supported by evidence on regional household patterns (see table 11).

These data illustrate two important points for under-

Table 11   Tejano and Anglo Household Types
by Region, 1850 and 1900

Household Types	Tejanos		Anglos	
	1850	1900	1850	1900
South Texas:				
Nuclear	94.0%	76.4%	75.9%	75.4%
Extended	5.0%	17.4%	1.2%	11.2%
Single Person	0.8%	5.9%	14.5%	11.4%
Undetermined	0.2%	0.3%	8.4%	2.0%
Sample Size	397	2593	84	399
Central Texas:				
Nuclear	60.4%	72.5%	73.4%	74.9%
Extended	35.5%	21.7%	20.4%	19.7%
Single Person	3.6%	5.3%	4.6%	4.4%
Undetermined	0.5%	0.5%	1.6%	1.0%
Sample Size	197	968	372	2060
West Texas:				
Nuclear	—	69.5%	—	72.6%
Extended	—	17.7%	—	11.0%
Single Person	—	11.8%	—	14.0%
Undetermined	—	1.0%	—	2.4%
Sample Size	—	994	—	947

Note: The sample sizes represent the number of households included
in the samples from the various sections for 1850 and 1900.

standing changes in Mexican household composition in
Texas between 1850 and 1900. First they indicate that
living arrangements were subject to variations based on
regional conditions. For example it can be seen in table 11
that extended-family households were much more prevalent at midcentury in central Texas than in the southern
region. Extended families occupied more than one-third
of Tejano households in central Texas, while about one-
fifth of Anglo households had this structure in 1850. In
the south extended families lived in only 5.0 percent of
the Tejano households and 1.2 percent of the white house-

holds. Nuclear-family households were almost universal among Mexicans in the southern region, and single-person households were more in evidence among Anglos. The fact that south Texas in 1850 was an established homeland for Mexicans and a new frontier for whites and the fact that central Texas was an urbanizing area with a more transient population makes direct sense of the facts of Tejano and Anglo household composition in the respective regions. Both Tejano and Anglo household and family arrangements were responding to regional differences in living conditions.

A second important point from table 11 concerns the very visible convergence of Mexican and Anglo household patterns between 1850 and 1900. In 1850 the lowest percentage of nuclear households was among central-Texas Mexicans (60.4 percent), and the highest was among Tejanos in south Texas (94.0 percent). Likewise the lowest percentage of single-person households was among Mexicans in central Texas (3.6 percent), and the highest was among whites in the southern region (14.5 percent). Wide differences in the percentages of extended-family households also existed at midcentury. However, as inspection of the data for 1900 shows, the large differences in household-composition patterns that existed both between regions and between ethnic groups in 1850 had disappeared by 1900. Both Mexicans and Anglos in the sections under study evidently experienced changes that strongly affected their lives. As Mexicans and Anglos adapted to new economic and social conditions during the drive toward modernity, their respective patterns of structuring households and families converged.

That Mexican-American households adapted to the changing conditions of nineteenth-century social life is a conclusion supported by mounting evidence from recent studies.[6] Elsewhere, for example, we have shown that Mexican marriage and childbearing behavior in Texas, as

well as patterns of financial dependence upon the gain-
fully employed members of Tejano households, changed
between 1850 and 1900 in a manner reflecting the influence of pressures caused by the transition from frontier to modernity.[7] Such findings point to the idea that
Mexican American families historically have adapted, as
have Anglo families, to surrounding life circumstances. In
the process a diversity of family types and behaviors has
emerged.[8]

Confirmation of this view, however, does not explain
all aspects of Mexican family life in Texas society. Important questions remain, specifically about the attitudes
of Anglos toward Tejanos and their families. How did
Anglo Americans envision the ways Tejanos conducted
their family life? What were the origins of their perceptions? What impact did they have on the place of Mexicans in mainstream Texas society? Did their attitudes
remain constant, or change over time?

Answering these questions, of course, goes beyond
the realm of statistical data derived from the federal censuses. Unlocking secrets of the heart and mind, discover-
ing the beliefs and feelings shared in common by people as
part of their culture, requires turning attention to sources
such as travel accounts, newspaper articles, and other
documents that reveal the inner thinking of Anglo Texans
during their encounters with Mexicans in the nineteenth
century. Fortunately several sources are available.[9]

Existing analyses, to be sure, have uncovered much
in the way of hostile attitudes toward Mexicans, but it is
a striking fact that they reveal little about white people's
views of such Tejano social institutions as the family. Of
all the documents, in other words, of all the observations
and tales recorded by early Anglo travelers to Texas, of all
the letters and personal papers written by white Texans,
of all the editorials and news articles churned from the
press, and of all the folklore from the tongues of Anglos

about Mexicans, none leaves a definitive image of what Anglos thought about the structure, the internal roles and relationships, the loyalties, obligations, goals, and routines of Tejano families. As one student of Texas family history has commented, "descriptions of Tejano families by Anglo travelers and settlers pictured only groups of people, often women and their children, without recognizing the structure and relationships that distinguish families in any culture." [10]

In the nineteenth century, there existed a void of commonly shared, clear, articulated views in Anglo culture, prejudicial or not, about Mexican-American families as such. The family as a social institution had little significance in the shared understandings of Anglos about the nature of Mexican life. More commonly the thoughts of whites expressed a range of racial and ethnic prejudices about the individual character traits of Mexicans.

Arnoldo De León, in *They Called Them Greasers*, has chronicled the attitudes of Anglos toward Mexicans in Texas for the period 1821–1900. De León's analysis reveals that the stereotypes and prejudices whites harbored were of several different varieties. First negative attitudes centered on Anglo interpretations of the physical traits of Tejanos. According to De León, "Uppermost among the things related to race that took up space in the writings of antebellum observers were the ancestry, bodily forms, and complexion of Tejanos." [11] The following views about Mexicans expressed by a prominent Brownsville resident in the 1860s exemplify this variant of Anglo prejudice: "They are of mongrel blood the Aztec predominating. These degraded creatures are mere pilferers, scavengers and vagabonds downright barbarians but a single remove above the Digger Indians, hanging like vermin on the skirts of civilization—a complete pest to humanity." [12]

Other strains of prejudice in the Anglo Texan community were less tangible. In contrast to those of an explicitly genetic nature, these lines of Anglo Texan thought focused on what whites saw as the habits of Mexicans. One theme that conveyed such ethnocentrism among whites, according to De León, was the perception that Mexicans were "an indolent people," whose traditions encouraged "docility, ignorance, decadence, mediocrity, antagonism toward work, submission to vice, and hedonistic proclivities." [13]

Mexicans were seen as people of "defective morality," and it was this strand of perceptions that touched most closely upon Tejano family life.[14] To be sure, in their thoughts about Mexican morality, Anglos made only indirect connections to the family. Anglo ideas of a century ago pictured Mexicans atomistically as individuals, not in terms of social units such as families. Still the perception of defective morality carried implications about family life precisely because, as De León recognized, "Whenever whites discussed the Mexicans' moral nature, references to sexuality punctuated their remarks." [15]

To an extent, such references expressed the attraction Anglo males felt toward Mexican *señoritas,* but beyond these sometimes tender feelings was a condemnation of Tejano capacities to establish and maintain "morally upright" marriages and families.[16] During the era of the republic in 1837, a visitor to San Antonio conveyed this attitude by observing that Mexicans had "less reserve and propriety in the manners and conduct of the different sexes in their intercourse with each other than would be tolerated in the States." [17] In the 1850s Frederick Law Olmsted, while acknowledging his attraction to the charms of Mexican women, wrote, "The constancy of the married women was made very light of, not that their favors were purchasable, they are sometimes seized by a strong penchant for some other than their lord." [18] Still later, in 1889, the *San Angelo Standard* reported that in the view of prominent citizens in that west-Texas

CHAPTER 5   community: ". . . [Mexican] mothers try hard to guard
their daughters until marriage, or at least to the time of
betrothal. Changing wives is not uncommon and neither
partner has much regard for the proprieties when living
together." [19]

Anglos in the nineteenth century had come to regard
Tejanos as morally loose and by implication incapable of
establishing stable family relations like those of whites.
But they perceived this moral defectiveness as a flaw of
the individual character of Mexicans, not as a deficiency
of the family seen as a social institution within their culture. Although it was manifest in the sexual habits of
Tejanos as interpreted by Anglos, it was a deeper inade-
quacy; one seen as endemic to the accidents of human
nature that made the Mexican people. In the minds of
whites, in other words, immorality was in the blood of
Mexicans, and this perception contributed to the denial
of room enough for Tejanos in Texas society. Their natural moral inferiority made the Tejanos unworthy of a free
and unbridled place of equal standing with whites in the
mainstream.

Still Anglos in the nineteenth century had not developed a full-fledged stereotype of the Mexican family as a
social institution. To phrase it another way, Anglos held
negative attitudes toward Tejanos as a category of individuals, but they had not yet formed the mind-set that
produced intense feelings of alienation toward the institutions of Mexican-American life. Why was this so? Why
did Anglos not have a clear perception of Tejano institutions such as the family in the nineteenth century? Why
did Anglos not develop such views until later?

An inquiry into these questions entails a deeper consideration of the nature of prejudice in the changing
society of Texas. The historian James E. Crisp raises some
of the complications involved in a paper entitled "Race,
Revolution, and the Texas Republic: Toward a Reinter-

pretation." In general Crisp's paper focuses on questions concerning the role of racism in the Texas war for independence, and advances the thesis that Anglo prejudice against Mexicans cannot be counted among the principal factors causing the break from Mexican rule in 1836. Instead, according to Crisp, "the Texas Revolution was less a consequence of racial friction than a precipitating cause of it," and "the greatest measure of oppression in Texas came not before 1836, but after."[20]

What is significant about Crisp's paper is not its central thesis concerning the role of racism in causing the Texas separation from Mexico. On that matter the authors align with David J. Weber who, in commenting on Crisp's paper, noted, "I agree . . . with Professor Crisp when he says ethnic conflict . . . was 'less a cause than a consequence of the [Texas] revolution,' but that does not mean that profound cultural and social differences did not play an important role in bringing on the revolution."[21]

Questions about the causes of Texas independence aside, what is important about Crisp's paper is its explicit counterposing of different historical forces involved in the evolution of prejudicial attitudes. On the one hand, Crisp bases his thesis on an "impressive body of historical and sociological scholarship indicating that the role of racism [in America] may be in large part epiphenomenal—a functional adjustment to changing circumstances rather than a principal causal factor in itself."[22] Stated in other terms, this means that prejudicial attitudes, in Crisp's view, are mental constructs that grow out of human relations, instead of factors involved in molding such relations. Thus Crisp espouses his agreement with the belief of the historian George M. Frederickson that "specific social and economic forces have been paramount in shaping [prejudice]."[23]

Opposing this point of view, says Crisp, are the perspectives of David J. Weber and Arnoldo De León. Their works of the early 1970s, according to Crisp, posited that prejudice was the underlying cause of the Texas war for independence. More recently, Crisp admits, Weber has conceded that such a view is insufficient, and presumably, only De León continues it.[24] In actuality Weber and De León hold that whites came to Texas with preconceptions about Mexican racial and cultural inferiority, and that these prejudices were among several factors causing the events of 1836.[25] Still counterposed in Crisp's paper are the opposing views that, on the one hand, racial and ethnic prejudice is a consequence of tension, competition, and conflict, but on the other, that prejudice is a factor in bringing about tensions, conflicts, and competition between racial and ethnic groups. Which is the case? Does prejudice result from clashes between groups, or is it a contributing cause?

A study of the negative images Anglos developed about Mexican Americans and their families suggests that both ideas are true. What appears to have happened in the evolution of a stereotype of the Tejano family is that negative attitudes harbored by Anglos in the nineteenth century, which incidentally abetted social inequality in that era, helped in important ways to shape relations between whites and Mexicans in a later era, the early twentieth century. Events in the later time, in turn, contributed to a perception of the Tejano family unit that had not existed earlier. But to repeat the previous question, why was the development of a clearly defined image of the Tejano family delayed until the twentieth century, when negative perceptions that impugned Mexicans as individuals existed in preceding decades?

We have seen repeatedly that the period between 1850 and 1900 was a time of transition in Texas. In general Anglos increased their dominance in the economic, political, and educational spheres of Texas society, while Tejanos experienced deterioration in their social standing. During this watershed of change, the shared beliefs of Anglos regarding Mexicans also changed.

In the nineteenth-century frontier era, not only was there a lack in Anglo Texan culture of any articulated imagery about the Mexican-American family as an institution, but there was a general absence of concepts about families in the cultures of all the main ethnic groups within the state. The folklorist Elizabeth York Enstam has observed that this era did not produce any myths or stereotypes about families of any sort. Not only was it the case that the Tejano family, considered as a social institution, was only vaguely comprehended in Anglo thoughts and attitudes about "defective Mexican morality," but Mexican Americans themselves never developed an image of the uniqueness of family life in their community. Neither, according to Enstam, did white Texans evolve any clear views of their families, nor did Indians or blacks in Texas. In Enstam's words, "The folklore of the four main Texas cultures [Indian, Mexican, black, and Anglo] exhibited little or no consciousness of the nature, purposes, or functions of family; family simply *was*."[26] Some reasons for this absence of perception, and thus of negative stereotyping, about families are poignantly mentioned by Enstam:

> In frontier times, Texas society in general was inhospitable to a real myth of family. While individual men undoubtedly treasured their homes and family relationships, . . . idealized visions of family were left to women. Home, after all, was woman's sphere. Most men, it would appear, took family for granted or saw their families as a means to specific ends. Men's interests, as a general rule, lay beyond the family in work or in the public realm. This was the separation of male and female spheres that people expected, with the men dominating public life and defining public policy. Thus, the values and goals of frontier Texas and of nineteenth century America, were not those of family, even though families provided the support sys-

tems and the means by which men's own plans would be accomplished.[27]

What was in the minds of Anglos in the frontier era, and not insignificantly Anglo men, as Enstam notes, was the task of establishing farms and ranches for a developing commercial economy, the challenge of building railroads and towns, founding new industries, erecting governments, and implementing public policies. Specifically when it came to feelings about Mexicans, what was in the forefront of Anglo thoughts corresponded to these frontier interests.

The most clearly articulated of negative Anglo images toward Mexicans, as chronicled by Arnoldo De León, explicitly had to do with the two areas of interest that most occupied the frontier Anglo mentality—economic and political matters.[28] In the realm of economics, it was the picture of idle and indolent Mexicans that was clear in the perceptions of whites. This was an image that nineteenth-century Anglos attributed to what they saw as the backward traditionalism of Mexicans, and they regularly contrasted it with the progressiveness of their own individual habits, as in the following account of an El Paso resident who in 1897 returned to the city after fifteen years of absence. The man recalled that what existed earlier was:

> . . . an adobe village which differed in no particular from like settlements in Mexico, and which gave no evidence to the traveler that he had emerged from the land of the Montezumas and that he was beneath the protecting folds of Old Glory. An adobe *jacal* was the leading hostelry of the place, it was presided over by a lazy Mexican and his still less industrious wife. The business houses were but rough buildings, of which the better grade were given up entirely to saloons and gambling dens. The streets were deep in sand, and the people apparently deep in thought, but thoughts which perhaps never led them to conceive

of any material change from their condition. [Now, however, the city stands as a monument] to the energy and
progressiveness of the American citizens, who, step by
step, starting at the Atlantic Ocean, overcoming every
obstacle, and facing every danger, have paved the dense
forests, mountain passes, and broad plains to the Pacific
with a civilization that stands without an equal in history.[29]

Curiously, in the sphere of politics, the vision of Mexicans that emerged in Anglo thinking was not one of idle-
ness and complacency, but rather one of active disloyalty
and subversion. According to De León, "The question of
Tejano patriotism came up often [during the nineteenth
century]."[30] From their suspected loyalty to Santa Anna
during the Texas war for independence to their antislavery
sentiments before the Civil War, and from the Cortina in-
surrection to the Cattle Wars of the 1870s, the Garza War,
and the Spanish American War, Anglos perceived in Tejanos a contempt for American civil law and a meddlesome
tendency toward subversion of public policies and institutions. In this realm as with economic matters, whites
articulated attitudes that typed Mexicans as distinctly un-
American, if not anti-American. David J. Weber's phrase
is appropriate for describing the seminal theme of Anglo
perceptions about Texas Mexicans during the frontier
era; they were seen as "foreigners in their native land."[31]

In the first three decades of the twentieth century,
Anglo Texans and Tejanos found themselves in a period
of economic development unmatched in the prior century. This period, sometimes described as the "Progressive Era," represents the other side of the drive toward
modernity that began in the previous century. The frontier became a memory, and a much-idealized one at
that. Now the economic advances made after 1850 continued to spread; industry and commerce expanded, railroad mileage increased measurably, commercial farming

replaced ranching in the agrarian sector, and cities took on twentieth-century trappings. New sources of capital and recent advances in technology brought a fresh wave of change in the early twentieth century, and accompanying it were a range of unexpected social pressures and issues.[32]

Among the new social forces affecting Anglo attitudes toward Tejanos after 1900 was the increased pace of Mexican immigration. In 1900 the census put the Mexican-born population of Texas at 71,062, but this was only the beginning. In the first decade of the century, Mexican immigration to Texas swelled so that the 1910 census placed the Mexican-born population at 125,016. In 1920 Mexican-born people numbered 251,827, and in 1930 there were 262,672 Mexican immigrants in the state.[33]

There is no doubt that economic change weighed heavily in the conditions drawing Mexican immigrants to the state. They left their homeland first because of the stresses of the Porfiriato and then because of the terror of the Revolution of 1910. But Texas, as well as other points in the southwest, pulled them because farmers and ranchers, businessmen and industrialists sought labor at lower wage rates than could otherwise be obtained in what was then an organizing and unionizing labor market.[34] As the historian Mario T. García has noted, "Hardworking and cheap, Mexican labor proved indispensable to employers." Yet, as Mexicans came in greater numbers, "increased cultural as well as social tensions . . . initiated efforts to 'Americanize' the Mexicans in the hope of making them more efficient and productive workers."[35]

It was in these changed conditions of the twentieth century in Texas that a perception of Tejano families, as families, took form in Anglo thinking. As Anglos sought to secure their economic interests by the importation of Mexican workers, they found themselves in greater contact with these people bearing a culture different from their own. That culture, it must be emphasized, was not new to Anglos, since they had encountered it upon their arrival in Texas a hundred years earlier. But for decades before, Anglo Texans and the state government had neglected the Tejano population. Entrenched, nineteenth-century attitudes had led them not to accommodate the ways of the Mexicans, but to see them as "foreign." Thus as early twentieth-century Anglos praised Mexicans for being hardworking and not susceptible to the intrusions of organized labor, they also suspected their capacity to follow steady, efficient, and productive work habits. More generally they doubted the ability of Mexicans to adapt to the modern industrial society and culture that had just arisen. In the Anglo view, after all, whites had brought Texas past the frontier into modernity, but Mexicans were still indolent and morally defective.[36]

But the changed realities of the early twentieth century forced Anglos to reconsider the place of Tejanos in Texas society. To an extent this led to increased opportunities. During World War I, for example, work-force shortages led officials to call upon the Texas Mexican community to become more actively involved in the war effort. Such overtures pointed in a direction of greater social integration and provided possibilities for Tejanos unavailable to them before.[37] On the other hand, the burgeoning Texas Mexican population caused what whites popularly came to see as the "Mexican Problem," and a concerted effort to "Americanize" Mexicans followed. In education, for example, the Mexican school-aged population increased to the extent that, by the 1920s, policymakers, school administrators, researchers, and teachers were consistently producing reports calling for action to promote educational reforms and legislative solutions to address this "Mexican Problem."[38]

Historically schooling was not developed for Mexicans. In the nineteenth century, the education of Mexicans met with neglect and discouragement. As school boards took new interest in Tejano students, they strove to achieve specific goals. Early twentieth-century schools in El Paso, for example, emphasized instruction in the manual and domestic skills needed for the low-level occupations that Anglos thought suitable for Mexicans. Also featured was education in the morals and values of American society, as whites saw them. Thus as early as 1904, the annual school report for the city incorporated the following comments concerning the "Mexican school":

> It is impossible to estimate the general good that this school is doing and has done among the benighted Mexican people . . . Yearly there are over six hundred children who attend regularly this school. They come from the humblest homes, where in years past, a knowledge of English and habits of cleanliness and refinement were unknown . . . Among the first lessons instilled into these children when they enter the school room is cleanliness. It is not an uncommon sight here to see a kind-hearted school marm standing in the lavatory room by one of these home neglected urchins, and supervising the process of bringing about conditions of personal cleanliness as he applys with vigor to rusty hands, dirty ears and neck, unkept face and head, the two powerful agencies of American civilization, soap and water.[39]

In this passage the evolution of a changing Anglo image of the Tejano family as a social institution is clear. No longer, by the early twentieth century, were Mexicans simply indolent and morally suspect. By this time in the perception of Anglos, Mexicans grew up in families where children were "home neglected urchins" and where "habits of cleanliness and refinement" went untaught. As Anglos intervened through "Americanization" in the transmission of what they came to see as deprived Mexican culture, they began stereotyping Tejano families as obstacles to the effort, blaming the family as a social unit for the perpetuation of flaws in the Mexican way of life.

This characterization subsequently flourished among Anglos, leading to a condemnation of the Mexican-American family as a source of Tejanos' criminality, poverty, failure in school, and resistance to acculturation and assimilation. Yet this Anglo image of Tejano families and the historical realities are at odds. The perception evolved early in the twentieth century, out of the combined influences of older nineteenth-century Anglo prejudices and the changed social conditions of the early 1900s. Meanwhile the historical realities of Mexican-American household and family patterns show adaptations to the transition toward modernity similar to those displayed by Anglo families. Indeed if the sociological consequences of stable families include the effective transmission of basic cultural principles from one generation to another, then Tejano families worked very well to preserve, adapt, and transmit a cultural heritage under difficult circumstances. Perhaps the real problem for Anglos is that Tejano families transmit the wrong culture, in their view. Texas has not, after all, been a land of room enough for accommodating its Mexican-American heritage. Anglos controlled economic, political, and social change in the nineteenth century, and their demeaning mind-set toward Mexicans justified exclusion and neglect of Tejanos. Changing conditions of modernization produced a reformulation of white prejudices. The revised, twentieth-century Anglo mentality about deprived Mexican culture and backward family life served to justify new, perhaps more intrusive, means of domination and discrimination.

Epilogue: Not Room Enough

Prior to the midnineteenth century, Texas stood as a challenging land of new beginnings for many peoples, nations, and civilizations. Tribal societies first sought to wrest their livelihood by a variety of means, ranging from plant cultivation to hunting and gathering. Centuries later came the Spanish conquest, resulting in the imposition of a complex European civilization, with its far-flung system of colonial governance, its precapitalist economic practices, and its culture infused with the influences of Iberian Catholicism. By virtue of an effort

93

to incorporate the indigenous peoples into their own ways, the Spaniards made a significant mark upon the history of Mexicans in Texas. Through intermixture and intermarriage, Spaniards begot a mestizo population that in time multiplied to form the cultural group of modern-day Tejanos. Indeed it was through this process that there emerged the "Mexican," as distinct from the Iberian "Spaniard," a new nation that eventually sought and gained independence from the colonial system.

Mexican rule over Texas, though short-lived, also had historically significant impacts on the history of Tejanos and the evolution of the social system of the state. During this era Tejanos devised plans to develop the state, both politically and economically, toward the fabric of a modern commercial and democratic society. But Anglos who entered the Tejas region at Mexico's invitation in the 1820s, to settle and defend the sparsely populated territory, turned events in another direction.

Upon gaining hegemony, Anglo Americans continued toward the goals that Mexicans had pursued between 1821 and 1836. However, the Anglo way of guiding the state's development not only resulted in a transition from frontier toward modernity, it also changed Texas into a land of not room enough. Tejanos under Anglo domination lost ground as whites gained it. Not only was this literally true, as Anglos seized control of Tejano lands, it was sociologically true in the system of labor and production, in politics, in education, and in the realm of cultural expression. In all these aspects of social life, the standing of Tejanos diminished through suppression and degradation. Our closing remarks aim to place the significance of such a history within the broader frameworks of Chicano studies and Texas scholarship.

Three significant forces shaped the Tejano community in the late nineteenth century: the establishment of American rule after 1836; immigration; and the transition toward modernity. The first of these set in motion a process of structural and ideological evolution that produced a dominant Anglo mind-set that was ethnocentric and racist in nature. Only by accepting the concept of Mexicans as a conquered people and a foreign group could Anglos have legitimated in their hearts and minds the displacement of Tejanos from the land and the economy. Within this same context, whites could feel justified in their manipulation and disenfranchisement of Tejanos in the political arena, in their neglect of them in the schooling process, and in their denigration of Mexican social life and culture.

Anglo attitudes and behavior, in turn, helped shape Tejano reactions toward whites. This was evident, for example, in the politics of the state, where Texas Mexicans pursued various strategies, ranging from the accommodationist style of José Antonio Navarro to the more aggressive and retaliatory stance of social rebels like Juan Cortina and Catarino Garza. Diverse as these approaches were, Tejano political efforts in the late nineteenth century shared the common aims of defending, preserving, and asserting the rights of Texas Mexicans against encroachments of Anglo-controlled and, to them, foreign institutions.

In addition to the conquest, immigration was a factor contributing to the development of Tejano life. That the phenomenon of incorporation by force is a fact of the history of Tejanos and Chicanos cannot be disputed. The annexation of the modern-day Southwest into the United States is a story of conquest, and many Mexican responses to Anglo-American society can be understood more fully by taking this into account.[1] But it is indisputable that Tejanos and Mexican Americans are, in ways that are crucial for understanding their history, immigrants to the United States.[2] Immigrants, by definition, are people who voluntarily cross international boundaries. They pull up stakes in one country and make an effort to sink new roots at some location in another nation. That some Tejanos and Chicanos are native to the Southwest and trace their ancestry and heritage to the region before its takeover by the United States is true enough. However, the majority are themselves, or are the descendants of, people who left Mexico to live in the United States after the Treaty of Guadalupe Hidalgo compelled Mexico to cede its lands in the far north to Anglo Americans.[3]

However, Tejanos and other Mexican Americans, by virtue of ironical turns in their history, are immigrants whose heritage and culture are native to the region where they have arrived. This irony, moreover, has exacerbated the perceptions of foreignness that have marked relations between Mexican Americans and Anglos through history.

Members of a host society usually see immigrants and their culture as foreign, and vice versa. Each experiences some degree of difficulty in identifying with the other. When immigrants enter with a desire to become part of the host society, they expect to cast off old ways and strive to acculturate and assimilate. But for Mexicans such has not been the case, for they have come as members of the Mexican culture that is indigenous to Texas and the Southwest. Again David J. Weber's phrase helps to describe such a turn of events; by conquest the Mexican way of life centered in the southwestern United States became a foreign culture in its own territory. Mexican immigrants have come as foreigners to a native land.[4]

If conquest, immigration, and accompanying feelings of alienation and foreignness worked their way into social relations between Anglos and Tejanos, a society undergoing transformation also helped to form the conduct of these two groups. The development of Texas from a frontier region toward a modern society during the nineteenth century entailed profound changes in the state's economy, including major effects on the composition of the labor force. With the rise of the commercial system, a whole range of skilled and specialized work roles endemic in the earlier localized, home-based, and self-sustaining production process dwindled away, to be replaced by an expanding demand for unspecialized, general laborers. The disproportionate concentration of Tejanos in the growing unspecialized labor pool was not, however, a necessary outcome of the economic transformation. This was more attributable to Anglo prejudices and discrimination, growing out of their perception of Tejano foreignness. Nonetheless it is clear that Anglos and Mexicans alike positively valued modernization, and many changes in the social patterns of both groups came in adapting to their differing circumstances within the transition toward modernity. Overall the present study of Mexicans in late-nineteenth-century Texas yields a picture of a diverse culture and community that actively adjusted its ways of life to conditions emanating from changes in the economic system and from the ironies of conquest and immigration that cast Tejanos as foreigners in their native land.

This portrayal of the Tejano community calls for a revision of our view of Mexican Americans as the subject matter of historical inquiry. In the 1980s Chicano scholars began depicting the Mexican-American community as socially and culturally diversified. Increasingly this is an underlying assumption of studies concerning the contemporary Mexican people of the United States.[5] Indeed the conquest, immigration, and the transition toward modernity all fueled a trend of diversification within the Tejano community. From the time of their incorporation into the United States, Tejanos manifested differences in their demographic and social characteristics, as well as in their political, economic, educational, household, and family orientations. Their community in the late nineteenth century, then, was not monolithic; it was diverse. It was not stagnant; it demonstrated dynamic change. Tejanos did

not strive to maintain archaic traditions; they were resilient in adapting to circumstances as changes unfolded.
Not only is the contemporary Tejano community a diverse and changing one; as a historical phenomenon, it is
a heritage of diversity and change.

Lastly this book calls for new understandings of Texas
history. Part of what is outlined in the text concerning
Texas in the nineteenth century is well known. For instance the development of the state's system of public education, in chapter four, is to be found in other writings,
as is the course of economic and political change outlined
in other chapters. These processes were involved in the
building and expansion of basic social institutions; and to
this history our contribution is modest. However, other
dimensions of Texas history are not as widely known.

In the textbook literature of Texas history, the emergence of the state's basic institutions, indeed the entire
transition toward modernity, is often portrayed as an
Anglo epic. It is a history, in other words, of white pio-
neers who came to Texas and threw off the yoke of an
oppressive Mexican government; who endured conflicts
with Mexicans and Indians; who engineered a merger
with the United States and took a stand in a civil war
between the states in an Anglo nation; who developed
cattle ranches and farms as well as towns and communities; who developed schools, built railroads, and formed
businesses, industries, and commercial enterprises. All of
this, according to the standard textbook view, organized
a vast frontier and defined a civilization that progressed
into the twentieth century. Mexicans (as well as other
minorities) are discussed as a separate group, peripheral
to the main progression of history, and often as people
who resisted and had to be overcome by steadfast whites
orchestrating the advancement toward modernity.[6]

Some elements of this textbook summary, of course,
have a basis in fact. It is true enough, for example, to say

that Anglos dominated the development of the state during the nineteenth century. Whites held the upper hand in the balance of military, political, economic, and social power. Change in social structures, therefore, was guided by Anglo concepts of such matters as business and commercial practices, the role of schooling in society, or the rights of individuals as citizens of the state. The values, beliefs, attitudes, norms, and customs of Anglo culture, in other words, shaped the course of Texas history because whites held the balance of power.

This, however, does not mean that Anglos were the only participants in the historical processes of the time. Nor does it mean that Mexicans lived as a peripheral group, resisting development and progress. To the contrary, our findings show that Mexicans played key roles in supplying labor for the expanding economy, that they participated actively in state and local politics and government, that they sought to advance their education where benefits followed, and that they adjusted and adapted their community and personal living situations to the demands and circumstances of development. Indeed it was Mexicans who first undertook a conscious effort to modernize the society of Texas; after the Texas war for independence in 1836, they maintained their ideals of progress and pursued them actively.

To portray the history of Texas as an epic of Anglos exclusively, then, is simply and purely an example of ethnocentrism. In actuality Texas history involves a plural society, constituted of men and women of many racial and ethnic origins who, under the domination of Anglo power, have been coparticipants in the development of the state. This study points out the need for further works on the pluralistic nature of Texas history as it involves the contributions and experiences of all its peoples.[7]

Also to be emphasized in further understanding the history of Texas is that, despite all its expanse of open space, all its resources, and the advances created in the transition begun in the nineteenth century, the state has not been a land of room enough for the aspirations of all its citizens. The frontier in much popular literature has been depicted as a place and time rich with opportunities and possibilities waiting to be seized by any one person with the brawn, brains, and fortitude to capture them. The individual's personal background was of no consequence, according to this myth, for the frontier beckoned rugged individuals with the talent and ability to build a civilization where only a wilderness came before. Truthfully, however, opportunity did not offer itself so readily. Rich as opportunities may have been, they provided the vehicle for only a few people to take direct action upon the great developments of the era. Most Texans of whatever color or creed lived in simple dwellings, had little contact with other than family members or immediate associates, and performed the on-going tasks of farming and ranching, carpentry, carting, laundry work, mining and smelting, laying railroad track, making saddles and shoes, or any one of a hundred other mundane occupations of ordinary people.

Our findings do not uphold the traditional image of Texas as a society of open, free, and equal opportunity. Anglos dominated the development of a new commercial economy and permitted Tejanos a niche only in the lowest-level service and general-labor occupations. Whites controlled a democratic government and limited the right of Tejanos to exercise civil liberties through manipulation and disenfranchisement. Anglos established a schooling system that neglected the education of Tejano children and dismissed the importance of what Mexicans learned in school. To be sure, Texans of all cultural persuasions could live free, according to their own standards of morality. But Anglos typed Tejanos as subhuman, indolent, subversive, morally defective, and foreign. The contributions of a plurality of peoples, different in their ethnic characteristics, brought about the changes of the nineteenth century, but Anglo Americans dominated positions of power and authority. They simply refused to make room enough for all the varied peoples of Texas.

Notes

Preface

1. An interesting discussion of the nuances of the concepts of industrialization and modernization as we use them is found in Peter L. Berger, Brigette Berger, and Hansfried Kellner, *The Homeless Mind: Modernization and Consciousness* (New York: Vintage Books, 1973), 3–20.

2. The phrase comes from the eminent historian John Hope Franklin, "The Land of Room Enough," *Daedalus* 110 (Spring 1981), 1–12. As a main theme of the book, "not the land of room enough" catches much of the irony involved in the history we examine.

3. Handwritten census schedules used between 1850 and 1900 listed about 40 persons per page. Thus a sample of 3,000 could be obtained from approximately 75 pages (40 time 75 equals 3,000). Consequently for counties over 12,000 population every "nth" page was sampled where "n" was determined by dividing the number of pages in the census report by 75. To illustrate, a county with a population of 28,000 would have about 700 pages in its census report. By dividing 700 by 75, it was determined that a sample of approximately 3,000 could be taken by covering every 9th page of the county's report.

4. These adjustments resulted from the sample-weighting system used for statistical analysis. Since evidence supported the assumption that samples were representative, the weighting system treated each sample as though it comprised 100 percent of the county's people in developing composite estimates of population characteristics. For example, the 1900 sample for Bexar County included 3,046 people from a total population of 69,422. By dividing the total population by the sample, it is determined that the

population was 22.79 times larger than the sample. By weighting the sample according to this factor, the sample could be treated as though it included the county's total population. Thus, the weight for the Bexar County sample in 1900 was 22.79. Composite estimates reported in this text reflect the weighting of all county samples according to this method unless otherwise indicated.

Chapter 1

1. See W. H. Timmons, *El Paso: A Borderlands History* (El Paso: University of Texas at El Paso Press, 1990), 18.

2. Carlos Eduardo Castañeda, *The Mission Era: The Winning of Texas, 1693–1751,* vol. 2 of *Our Catholic Heritage in Texas, 1519–1936* (7 vols., Austin: Boeckmann-Jones Company, 1936; reprinted New York: Arno Press, 1976), 46 n. 22, 47, 59–60.

3. Jesús F. de la Teja, "Forgotten Founders: The Military Settlers of Eighteenth-Century San Antonio de Béxar," in Gerald E. Poyo and Gilberto M. Hinojosa, *Tejano Origins in Eighteenth-Century San Antonio* (Austin: University of Texas Press, 1991), 29; and Gerald E. Poyo, "Immigrants and Integration in Late Eighteenth-Century Béxar," ibid., 85.

4. Poyo, "The Canary Islands Immigrants of San Antonio: From Ethnic Exclusivity to Community in Eighteenth-Century Béxar," ibid., 47; Poyo, "Immigrants and Integration," 86, 87; Gilberto M. Hinojosa and Anne A. Fox, "Indians and Their Culture in San Fernando de Béxar," ibid., 106, 107; and Alicia V. Tjarks, "Comparative Demographic Analysis of Texas, 1777–1793," *Southwestern Historical Quarterly* 77 (January 1974) 322–28.

5. Terry G. Jordan, *Trails to Texas: Southern Roots of Western Ranching* (Lincoln: University of Nebraska Press, 1981), 108.

6. Jack Jackson, *Los Mesteños: Spanish Ranching in Texas, 1721–1821* (College Station: Texas A & M University Press, 1986), 52, 92.

7. Martín Salinas, *Indians of the Río Grande Delta: Their Role in the History of Southern Texas and Northeastern Mexico* (Austin: University of Texas Press, 1990), 17–20; Gilberto M. Hinojosa, *A Borderlands Town in Transition: Laredo, 1755–1870* (College Station: Texas A & M University Press, 1983), 5–9; Paul S. Taylor, *An American Mexican Frontier: Nueces County Texas* (Chapel Hill: University of North Carolina Press, 1934), 9–12.

8. Timmons, *El Paso,* chap. 2.

9. David J. Weber, *The Mexican Frontier, 1821–1846: The American Southwest under Mexico* (Albuquerque: University of New Mexico Press, 1982), 16, 21–22.

10. Jaime E. Rodríguez-O, "La Constitución de 1824 y la formación del Estado Mexicano," *Historia Mexicana* 40 (January/February 1991) 518, 525, 530.

11. Weber, *Mexican Frontier*, 160.

12. Ibid., 158–61.

13. Poyo, "The Canary Islands Immigrants of San Antonio," in Poyo and Hinojosa, *Tejano Origins*, 56, 138.

14. Jackson, *Los Mesteños*, 596–97.

15. Jesús F. de la Teja and John Wheat, "Béxar: Profile of a Tejano Community, 1820–1832," *Southwestern Historical Quarterly* 89 (July 1985) 26, 28.

16. Jackson, *Los Mesteños*, 592.

17. Taylor, *American Mexican Frontier*, 10–13.

18. Hinojosa, *Borderlands Town*, 42.

19. Weber, *Mexican Frontier*, 176.

20. de la Teja and Wheat, "Béxar," 30–31.

21. Randolph B. Campbell, *An Empire for Slavery: The Peculiar Institution in Texas* (Baton Rouge: Louisiana State University Press, 1989), 23–24.

22. Juan N. Almonte, "Statistical Report on Texas," trans. by C. E. Castañeda, *Southwestern Historical Quarterly* 28 (January 1925) 201, 207; see also Ohland Morton, *Terán and Texas: A Chapter in Texas-Mexican Relations* (Austin: Texas State Historical Association, 1948), 59–62.

23. These population figures come from Weber, *The Mexican Frontier*, 177.

24. Barnes F. Lathrop, *Migration into East Texas, 1835–1860* (Austin: Texas State Historical Association, 1949), 60.

25. Ibid., 27.

26. *Historical Statistics of the United States: Colonial Times to 1970* (Washington, D.C.: U.S. Bureau of the Census, 1975) 1:93.

27. The national increase between 1850 and 1900 was from 23 million to 76 million, a growth of about 230 percent. In Texas the population grew from some 213,000 to over 3 million, an increase of about 1,331 percent. See ibid. 1:8, 35; see also Terry G. Jordan, *Immigrants to Texas* (Boston: American Press, 1981), 5–7.

28. Estimates of the 1836 Texas population are greatly divergent. The lower estimate given here is from D. W. Meinig, *Imperial Texas: An Interpretive Essay in Cultural Geography* (Austin: Uni-

versity of Texas Press, 1969), 31. The higher one is given by Seymour V. Connor, *Texas: A History* (Arlington Heights, Ill.: Harlan Davidson, 1971), 173. The 1900 figure is from the *United States Census of Population*, ser. nos. 1850.1–1900.22, microfilmed from the holdings of the Social and Economic Statistics Administration Library (formerly the Bureau of the Census Library), Suitland, Maryland (New Haven: Research Publications), 1900.1, p. xviii. A lower count of 3,049,000 for 1900 is found in *Historical Statistics of the United States* 1:35.

29. Terry G. Jordan, "The Imprint of the Upper and Lower South on Mid-Nineteenth Century Texas," *Annals of the Association of American Geographers* 57 (1967) 667–90; and Jordan, "Population Origins in Texas, 1850," *The Geographical Review* 59 (January 1969) 83–103.

30. These include Alabama, Florida, Georgia, Louisiana, Mississippi, and South Carolina.

31. The upper southern states are Arkansas, The District of Columbia, Kentucky, Maryland, Missouri, North Carolina, Tennessee, and Virginia (including West Virginia).

32. These figures derive from information available in *Historical Statistics of the United States* 1:458–64. The same information shows that Texas farms accounted for about 1% of the total value of United States farmland and buildings in 1850.

33. Texas farms in 1850 averaged 943 acres; the average number of acres per farm in the United States was 203. Although farms were large by comparison, a simple comparison of cotton yields in Texas and the nation illustrates their low productivity. Cotton was the major cash crop in midcentury Texas; the yield was over 57,000 bales in 1850. That amounts to about one bale for every 202 acres of farmland in the state. Nationwide, the 1850 cotton yield was about 2.1 million bales; about one bale for every 137 acres of U.S. farmland. Comparison of cotton production in Texas with that of southern states would result, of course, in a much larger difference. For useful acreage and cotton-production statistics in 1850, see ibid. 1:458–64, 517–18.

34. *U.S. Census of Population*, 1850.1, 514–20.

35. It should be acknowledged that political and military circumstances in south Texas prior to 1850 were not conducive to agricultural development such as that in other regions of the state. Between 1836 and 1845, it was a disputed territory. The Republic of Texas and Mexico both claimed sovereignty over it. Then the ravages of the Mexican War came to the region between 1846

and 1848. Political uncertainties and military disruption may help to explain the relative paucity of agricultural advancement, but the fact remains that it was this region of predominantly Mexican population that did not share in the early development of the Texas farming economy. The benefits of development coincided with regional ethnicity.

36. Kenneth M. Wheeler, *To Wear a City's Crown: The Beginnings of Urban Growth in Texas, 1836–1865* (Cambridge, Mass.: Harvard University Press, 1968), 150–66; and John W. Reps, *Cities of the American West: A History of Frontier Urban Planning* (Princeton, N.J.: Princeton University Press, 1979), 593, 595, 610, 614, 618.

37. Meinig, *Imperial Texas*, 68, 71–72.

38. David Montejano, *Anglos and Mexicans in the Making of Texas, 1836–1986* (Austin: University of Texas Press, 1987), 89, 91, 92.

39. See *U.S. Census of Population,* 1900.4–5, Report 229; 1900.4–3, Report 146.

40. John S. Spratt, *The Road to Spindletop: Economic Change in Texas, 1875–1901* (Dallas: Southern Methodist University Press, 1955), 302, citing *U. S. Census,* 1900 viii: Manufacturers, 863.

Chapter 2

1. The total increase in farm acreage between 1850 and 1900 was 114.3 million acres, about 88 percent of which came into use after 1870. The fifty-year increase in the number of manufacturing establishments was 11,980, with 83 percent of these founded between 1870 and 1900. The annual value of farm products increased by some $238 million between 1850 and 1900, with about 84 percent of this growth after 1870. Manufactured products increased in annual value by some $118 million, about 91 percent coming in the decades after the Civil War. See *U.S. Census of Population,* 1850.1, p. 209; 1900.4–3, Report 146; and 1900.4–5, Report 229.

2. The growth of industry around the state's major urban centers is described in Vera Lea Dugas, "Texas Industry, 1860–1880," *Southwestern Historical Quarterly* 59 (October 1955) 151–83. See also Christopher S. Davies, "Life at the Edge: Urban and Industrial Evolution of Texas, Frontier Wilderness—Frontier Space, 1836–1986," *Southwestern Historical Quarterly* 89 (April 1986) 443–554.

3. In other works we have focused on subregions within the

Mexican settlement region in an effort to determine unfolding processes during the era. Readers wishing to know how economic circumstances affected laborers in south, central and west Texas are referred to Arnoldo De León, *The Tejano Community, 1836–1900,* with a contribution by Kenneth L. Stewart (Albuquerque: University of New Mexico Press, 1982), chapters 3 and 4; De León and Stewart, *Tejanos and the Numbers Game: A Socio-Historical Interpretation from the Federal Censuses, 1850–1900* (Albuquerque: University of New Mexico Press, 1989), 104 n. 7; De León and Stewart, "Lost Dreams and Found Fortunes: Mexican and Anglo Immigrants in South Texas, 1850–1900," *Western Historical Quarterly* 14 (July 1983) 291–310; De León and Stewart, "Tejano Demographic Patterns and Socio-Economic Development: A Research Note," *Borderlands Journal* 7 (Fall 1983) 1–9; and De León and Stewart, "Work Force Participation among Mexican Immigrant Women in Texas, 1900," *Borderlands Journal* 9 (Spring 1986) 69–74.

4. It should be noted that while the proportion of workers involved in manufacture and mechanical pursuits showed a net 1.8 percent decrease over the last fifty years of the nineteenth century, the category increased in the postbellum period. The decline between 1860 and 1870 was probably due to the demise of "home manufacturing" industries, which were an important part of the more self-sufficient Texas economy before the war. The increase in the postbellum period was the result of the expansion of industrial manufacturing establishments.

5. Study of the spread of manufacturing establishments in nineteenth-century Texas shows that enterprises relied on a strong agricultural base. In 1900, for example, seven of the ten leading industries (as measured by the dollar value of their products) were directly dependent on the fruits of the land for raw materials, including lumber and timber products, cottonseed oil and cake, flour and gristmill products, cotton ginning, saddlery and harness, liquor products, and lumber-mill products. This, of course, meant that industrial establishments were likely to take root and survive in those areas where agricultural productivity was strongest. In both 1850 and 1900, seven of the state's top fifteen industrial counties (again as measured by the dollar value of manufactured products) were among the top fifteen in agricultural products. The close association between agricultural and industrial productivity helps explain why the Mexican settlement region was later in developing a manufacturing sector. It also helps to explain why the industries that did come to the region were of a larger scale compared to those in

other areas of the state. The larger scale is shown by the fact that in 1900 the average capital investment per establishment in the Mexican region was about $3,000 more than the state's fifteen leading industrial counties. The Mexican region simply did not have the diverse and productive agricultural base that would support a variety of profitable small-scale manufacturing establishments. As local markets opened to more distant commercial suppliers, the home industries declined as elsewhere, and industries of relatively large scale, but few in number, were the remaining source of demand for manufacturing and mechanical labor. See *U.S. Census of Population,* 1850.1, pp. 514, 520; 1850.2, pp. 310–19; 1900.4–3, Report 146; and 1900.4–5, Report 229.

6. This 8.7 percent decline in the proportion of trade and transportation workers was also in contrast to the state as a whole, where there was a 6.3 percent increase in the category; see table 5.

7. In exact terms the sample data from twenty south-, central-, and west-Texas counties indicates that only 9.5 percent of the service workers in 1850 fell into the personal-service side of the category; 90.5 percent were in professional employments. These proportions changed to 55.7 percent and 44.3 percent, respectively, by 1880. By 1900 personal-service workers comprised 66 percent of the category, and professionals had dwindled to 34 percent.

8. The combination of increasing Anglo and decreasing Tejano agricultural employment corresponds to the dispossession of Mexicans from the land. According to the sample information from twenty counties in the Mexican settlement region, some 35 percent of Tejano workers owned or controlled land used for farming and stockraising in 1850; only 11 percent of the Anglo labor force was similarly situated. By 1900, however, these proportions had reversed. Tejano farmers and stockraisers made up only 17 percent of the Mexican labor force, while the number of Anglos so employed had climbed to 26 percent. For descriptions of the dispossession of Tejanos from the land, see De León and Stewart, "Lost Dreams," 291–310; and David Montejano, *Anglos and Mexicans.*

9. The sample data from the Mexican settlement region indicate that 83.2 percent of the Tejanos in service pursuits in 1900 were in the personal services; only 16.8 percent had attained professional status. About 36.9 percent of the total personal-service labor force consisted of obreros while about 15.5 percent of the region's professional workers were Mexican Americans. Anglos, on the other hand, comprised about 75.3 percent of the professional ranks and some 29.0 percent of the personal-service workers.

10. Variations on this pattern of subjugation of Tejano labor

occurred in different parts of the region. It was most severe in central Texas, where Anglos constituted a numerical majority of the population by 1900. Sample data from seven counties in the area show that obreros held their own in the agricultural sector but experienced sharp reductions in trade, transportation, and manufacturing opportunities. In 1850 about 77 percent of Mexican-American workers in central Texas were employed in these categories; only 5.7 percent were in 1900. Tejanos involved in unspecified labor pursuits increased from 18 percent to 68.2 percent in the same time period. Information from five south-Texas counties shows that Tejanos lost opportunities there in the agricultural and manufacturing realms. Some 54 percent of them were working in agriculture in 1850, and another 43.3 percent engaged in manufacturing. These proportions dwindled to 17.3 percent and 8.2 percent respectively by 1900. The number involved in unspecified labor mushroomed from less than 1 percent to 46.4 percent in the southern area. West Texas seems to have been less harsh in excluding Tejanos from job opportunities; in this area the proportion of Mexican Americans in agriculture declined by about 10 percent between 1860 and 1900, and a reduction of 2 percent occurred in manufacturing employments. Nevertheless the number of Tejanos in unspecified labor roles in west Texas increased from 30 percent to 45 percent in the forty years between 1860 and 1900.

11. See De León and Stewart, "Lost Dreams," and Montejano, *Anglos and Mexicans,* 50–74. See also Mario Barrera, *Race and Class in the Southwest: A Theory of Racial Inequality* (Notre Dame, Ind.: University of Notre Dame Press, 1979), 34–37. The mechanisms of occupational discrimination and repression are an overriding focus of the sections on Chicano labor in Rodolfo Acuña, *Occupied America: A History of Chicanos* (3d ed.; New York: Harper and Row, 1988).

12. For an account of attitudes toward Mexican servants in Corpus Christi, see Mary A. Sutherland, *The Story of Corpus Christi,* ed. by Frank B. Harrison (Houston: Rein and Sons, 1916), 84–85. The Pleasanton sheepraiser's comments can be found in the San Antonio *Express,* 12 March 1879, p. 4; and examples of advertisements featuring the cheap Mexican labor of south Texas are from the San Antonio *Express,* 4 December 1877, p. 2; and the Corpus Christi *Weekly Caller,* 15 March 1885, pp. 2, 4. See also the discussion in Emilio Zamora, "Mexican Labor Activity in South Texas, 1900–1920" (Ph.D. diss. University of Texas at Austin, 1983), 51–52. That the desire to keep Mexicans in a low

occupational niche extended even into the twentieth century is illustrated in a 1937 newspaper article entitled "Texas Relief Rolls Cut to Bone as Task of Harvesting Big Cotton Crop is Begun." This article accompanied an advertisement from plantation owners in Gonzales County warning against attempts to lure cotton pickers away from the area with higher-paying jobs. See the San Angelo *Standard-Times*, 8 August 1937, p. 3.

13. According to various accounts, some Mexicans in fact did move. On the eve of the Civil War, for example, Tejano cartmen traveled as far north as Dallas to buy flour, and similar trade expeditions continued in the postbellum period. See Shirley Achor, *Mexican Americans in a Dallas Barrio* (Tucson: University of Arizona Press, 1978), 56; and De León, *Tejano Community*, 63–65. On the early presence of Mexicans on the Gulf Coast of east Texas, see Arnoldo De León, *Ethnicity in the Sunbelt: A History of Mexican Americans in Houston, Texas* (Houston: Mexican American Studies Program, University of Houston, 1989).

14. Neil F. Foley, "Chicanos and the Culture of Cotton in South Texas, 1880–1900: Reshaping Class Relations in the South," in Mary Romero and Cordelia Candelaria, eds., *Community Empowerment and Chicano Scholarship* (Los Angeles: National Association for Chicano Studies, 1992), 112.

15. See Achor, *Mexican Americans*, 57; and De León, *Ethnicity in the Sunbelt*.

16. A more complete discussion of anti-Mexican sentiment in the antebellum period is found in Arnoldo De León, *They Called Them Greasers: Anglo Attitudes toward Mexicans in Texas* (Austin: University of Texas Press, 1983).

17. Dallas *Weekly Herald*, 9 March 1878, p. 4. Other examples of the same preference are expressed in issues of the same paper on 29 December 1877, p. 2; and 12 January 1878, p. 2.

18. San Antonio *Express*, 28 December 1897, p. 1; and 9 March 1898, p. 5. In the 1930s farmers in this same area went to quite the opposite extreme of putting up signs warning whites not to block Mexican cotton pickers from going to work in the fields. Apparently they were having to undo earlier patterns of exclusion. See the San Angelo *Standard Times*, 8 August 1937, p. 3.

19. See *U.S. Census of Population*, 1890.2, pp. 448–53; and 1900.18, pp. 392–97, 612–13.

20. These are rates for farm laborers without board. The rates for those receiving board with the job were $1.32 and $.93 in 1866 and 1899, respectively. According to the Industrial Commission

report, similar declines in farm-labor wages occurred in most of the United States, a fact that the Commission attributed to deflation of currency in the decades after the Civil War. See *Report of the Industrial Commission on Agriculture and on Taxation in Various States,* vol. 11 (Washington, D.C.: U.S. Government Printing Office, 1901), 87–143.

21. See the excellent discussion of national and regional trends in farm-labor wages and cost of living in Fred A. Shannon, *The Farmer's Last Frontier: Agriculture, 1860–1897,* vol. 5 of *The Economic History of the United States* (New York: Holt, Rinehart and Winston, 1945), 359–67.

22. Zamora, "Mexican Labor Activity," 45.

23. See *U.S. Census of Population, 1900.*4–3, Report 146, p. 3.

24. It should be noted that manufacturing labor is generally less seasonal than farm work. Thus the annual earnings of workers in manufacturing were probably far greater than what their agricultural counterparts took home, even though monthly wages in manufacturing were not appreciably higher.

25. Although the available information precludes substantiating this on the basis of data regarding Texas specifically, national studies of wage differences show considerable discrepancies between skilled and unskilled manufacturing employees. A national survey of forty-eight flour and gristmills and ten brick manufacturing establishments in 1880 indicated that general laborers in those industries earned daily wages of about $1.26 and $1.32, respectively. Over a thirty-day period, this adds up to monthly wages of $37.80 and $39.60. In contrast the average daily wages of skilled workers in the same industries ranged from $1.86 for molders in brick making to $3.33 for millwrights in flour and gristmill operations. The earnings of skilled workers in the two industries thus appear to have ranged from 48 percent to 152 percent higher than those of general day laborers in the same establishments. See *U.S. Census of Population, 1880.*11, pp. 29–34. Other evidence reported by Clarence D. Long, *Wages and Earnings in the United States, 1860–1890* (New York: National Bureau of Economic Research, 1960), 144, shows that the average daily wages of blacksmiths, carpenters, engineers, machinists, and painters in manufacturing establishments across the nation were consistently from 55 percent to 85 percent higher than the rates for general manufacturing labor between 1860 and 1880.

26. *U.S. Census of Population,* 1900.4–3, Report 146, p. 3.

27. The Census Bureau ceased the practice of inquiring into the wealth of individuals in 1880. Thus statistics of wealth for the decades after 1870 are unavailable.

28. These and other calculations presented here are based on sample information classified by the Census Bureau under the label "Value of Personal Estate." The bureau also collected information on the "Value of Real Estate" holdings, but those data are much less complete and subject to greater degrees of invalidity. The counties in south and central Texas included in the 1850 sample were Bexar, Cameron, Guadalupe, Nueces, Starr, and Webb. The 1870 sample includes these plus Duval county in south Texas; Atascosa, Bee, Karnes, Travis, and Victoria counties in the central part of the state; and El Paso and Presidio counties in west Texas. Sample data on 345 obreros and 719 Anglo workers residing in six south- and central-Texas counties in 1850 reveal that the two groups had amassed combined assets of some $965,518 in personal wealth by that year. Another sample of 4,565 Tejano and Anglo laborers from fourteen counties in the Mexican settlement region of Texas in 1870 yielded a combined worth of $2,517,205.

29. The notion that Mexicanos inclined toward extended-family arrangements is not born out by the data. The sample information shows that about 78 percent of the 1850 Tejano population lived in households occupied by nuclear families. The proportion in 1900 was 89 percent. In contrast only about 67 percent of Anglos lived in nuclear-family households in 1850, although this increased to match the figure for Tejanos by 1900.

30. Comparable figures for the Anglo population were as follows: (a) 45 percent of the 1850 Anglo labor force was made up of male household heads; (b) working spouses and children accounted for 2.8 percent; (c) the 1900 laboring population of Anglos was composed of 60 percent male heads of households; (d) 24 percent of the workers in 1900 were spouses and children: (e) the proportion of working spouses among Anglos declined slightly from 2.7 percent to 2.2 percent between 1850 and 1900; and (f) working children increased from 1.2 percent in 1850 to 13.8 percent in 1900.

31. Montejano, *Anglos and Mexicans,* 110; see also 76, 79–84, 104.

Chapter 3

1. Alfredo Cuellar, "Perspective on Politics," in Joan W. Moore with Alfredo Cuellar, *Mexican Americans* (Englewood Cliffs, N.J.: Prentice-Hall, 1970), 137–58.

2. Examples of views felt to be in need of correction at the time of Cuellar's writing are Edgar Greer Shelton, *Political Conditions among Texas Mexicans along the Río Grande* (San Francisco: R&E Research Associates, 1974), and Ozzie G. Simmons, *Anglo-Americans and Mexican Americans in South Texas* (New York: Arno Press, 1974).

3. David Montejano, *Anglos and Mexicans*, 34, 39–49, 94–95, 129.

4. Likewise no Tejano candidate won a federal office in the nineteenth century.

5. These were Basilio Benavides, Santos Benavides, J. A. Chavis [sic], Gregorio N. García, Angel Navarro, T. A. Rodríguez, and T. P. Rodríguez.

6. For a listing of the members of these nineteenth-century legislatures, see Texas Legislature, *Members of the Texas Legislature, 1846–1962* (Austin: Fifty-Seventh Legislature, 1962), 3–184.

7. The multiplication of local governments in the last three decades of the century is shown by the fact that six of the twenty counties that were sampled to obtain quantitative data for this study did not exist as political jurisdictions before 1870. Of these, Crockett, Pecos, and Tom Green counties were established in the 1870s; Crane, Sutton, and Val Verde in the 1880s.

8. For Barr's commentary on the growing significance of local politics, see Alwyn Barr, *Reconstruction to Reform: Texas Politics, 1876–1906* (Austin: University of Texas Press, 1971), 15–16, 203. See also, Montejano, *Anglos and Mexicans*, 133–35, and Douglas E. Foley et al., *From Peones to Politicos: Ethnic Relations in a South Texas Town, 1900–1977*, 2d ed. (Austin: Center for Mexican American Studies, University of Texas, 1988), 19–20.

9. De León, *The Tejano Community*, chapter 1. See also Mario T. García, *Desert Immigrants: The Mexicans of El Paso, 1880–1920* (New Haven: Yale University Press, 1981), chapter 8; and Montejano, *Anglos and Mexicans*, pp. 34, 39–49, 94–95, 129. In addition the political incumbency of Tejanos in post–Civil War Laredo receives attention in Roberto R. Calderón, "The Mexican Electorate and Politics in South Texas, 1865–1881" (paper

presented at the XVI National Association for Chicano Studies Conference, Boulder, Colo., 14–16 April 1988).

10. De León, *The Tejano Community,* 33–34; Montejano, *Anglos and Mexicans,* 40.

11. In other works, we have focused on subregions within the Mexican settlement region in an effort to determine unfolding processes during that era. Readers wishing to know more of politics in south, central, and west Texas are referred to De León, *The Tejano Community,* chapter 2. Of related interest is De León, "The Tejano Experience in Six Texas Regions," *West Texas Historical Association Yearbook;* 65 (1989) 36–49.

12. De León, *Tejano Community,* chapter 2.

13. Montejano, *Anglos and Mexicans,* 36–37; Robert J. Rosenbaum, *Mexicano Resistance in the Southwest: "The Sacred Right of Self-Preservation"* (Austin: University of Texas Press, 1981), 42.

14. Juan Cortina still awaits a definitive biography. For coverage of the historical literature on him, see Jerry Don Thompson, "The Many Faces of Juan Nepomuceno Cortina," *South Texas Studies,* vol. 2 (Victoria, Texas: Victoria College Press, 1991), 85–98.

15. James Ridley Douglas, "Juan Cortina: El Caudillo de la Frontera" (M.A. thesis, University of Texas at Austin, 1987), 66, 70, 132. See also Walter L. Buenger, *Secession and the Union in Texas* (Austin: University of Texas Press, 1984), 90–91; and Montejano, *Anglos and Mexicans,* 36.

16. Works touching on the life of José Antonio Navarro include Joseph Martin Dawson, *José Antonio Navarro: Co-Creator of Texas* (Waco: Baylor University Press, 1969); James Ernest Crisp, "Anglo-Texan Attitudes toward the Mexicans, 1821–1834" (Ph.D. diss., Yale University, 1976), 399–403, 408–50; and Walter L. Buenger, *Secession and the Union,* 85, 90–91, 95, 104.

17. Rodolfo Acuña, "The Making of *Occupied America,*" in Tatcho Mindiola, ed., *Occupied America: A Chicano History Symposium,* monograph 3 (Houston: Mexican American Studies Program, University of Houston, 1982), 23.

18. Crisp, "Anglo-Texan Attitudes" 336, 350–51, 408.

19. Aspects of Santos Benavides's life are documented in John Denny Riley, "Santos Benavides: His Influence on the Lower Río Grande, 1823–1891" (Ph.D. dissertation, Texas Christian University, 1976); L. E. Daniell, *Types of Successful Men of Texas*

(Austin: publ. by the author, Eugene Von Boeckman, Printer and Bookbinder, 1890), 324–30, and Hinojosa, *A Borderlands Town in Transition*, 77, 82–86. Benavides's military career is covered in Jerry Don Thompson, *Vaqueros in Blue and Gray* (Austin: Presidial Press, 1976).

20. Riley, "Santos Benavides," 256–57, 263–64; Montejano, *Anglos and Mexicans*, 36.

21. There are no significant English-language documentary sources for Catarino Garza. Works in Spanish include Gabriel Saldívar, *Documentos de la rebelión de Catarino E. Garza en la Frontera de Tamaulipas y sur de Texas, 1891–1892* (Mexico City: Secretaría de Agricultura y Fomento, 1943). Some of Garza's personal papers are deposited at the Mexican American Archives, Benson Latin American Collection, University of Texas, Austin.

22. For an excellent analysis of the "social bandit" in the American West see Richard White, "Outlaw Gangs of the Middle Border: American Social Bandits," *Western Historical Quarterly* 12 (October 1981) 387–408. Garza's place in Mexican-American folklore is told in Américo Paredes, *A Texas-Mexican Cancionero: Folksongs of the Lower Border* (Urbana: University of Illinois Press, 1976), 28–30. Biographical sketches are found in Gilbert M. Cuthbertson, "Catarino Garza and the Garza War," *Texana* 12 (1974) 335–48; and Agnes G. Grimm, *Llanos Mesteñas: Mustang Plains* (Waco: Texian Press, 1968), 139–45.

23. Evan Anders, *Boss Rule in South Texas: The Progressive Era* (Austin: University of Texas Press, 1982), chapter 3; Montejano, *Anglos and Mexicans*, 130, 139.

24. Anders, *Boss Rule in South Texas*, 12–14. See also Montejano, *Anglos and Mexicans*, 39–40, 110.

25. The idea that bossism in American politics was an outgrowth of the failure of the political process to serve as an effective means of realizing the goals of political activity among disadvantaged groups was set forth by Robert K. Merton, *Social Theory and Social Structure* (Glencoe, Ill.: Free Press, 1957), 70–81. Studies advancing this view include Joel A. Tarr, *A Study of Boss Politics: William Lorimer of Chicago* (Chicago: University of Illinois Press, 1971); Zane Miller, *Boss Cox's Cincinnati: Urban Politics in the Progressive Era* (New York: Oxford University Press, 1968); Seymour Mendelbaum, *Boss Tweed's New York* (New York: John Wiley and Sons, 1965); and John M. Allswang, *Bosses, Machines, and Urban Voters: An American Symbiosis* (Port Washington, N.Y.: Kennikat Press, 1977).

The borrowed phrase is from William Ryan, *Blaming the Victim* (New York: Pantheon Books, 1971). Ryan argues that a standard technique in American efforts at dealing with social problems has been to displace attention from needed reforms in institutions by "blaming the victims" for the problems to which they are subjected. This thesis seems appropriate to the idea that Tejanos were subjected to boss rule because of an unsubstantiated cultural preference for feudalistic practices.

26. See for example Poyo, "The Canary Islands Immigrants," 53–56, 58; and Rodríguez-O, "La Constitución de 1824," 518.

27. For an extensive analysis of the nature of the Spanish-Mexican political heritage, see J. H. Parry, *The Spanish Seaborne Empire* (New York: Alfred A. Knopf, 1966).

28. Alexis de Toqueville, *Democracy in America,* ed. by J. P. Mayer, trans. by George Lawrence (Garden City, N.Y.: Doubleday and Company, 1969).

29. De León, *They Called Them Greasers.*

Chapter 4

1. Though not specific to the transformation that occurred in Texas society in the last half of the nineteenth century, an excellent general analysis of the affinities between modernization and public school systems is found in Val D. Rust, *Alternatives in Education: Theoretical and Historical Perspectives,* Sage Studies in Social and Educational Change, vol. 6 (Beverly Hills: Sage Publications, 1977).

2. Michael Allen White, "History of Education in Texas, 1860–1884" (Ed.D. diss., Baylor University, 1969) provides a detailed account of political developments in this period that helped to gain popular support in the state for the establishment of a free public education system. The most widely read volumes on the history of the Texas school system are Frederick Eby, *The Development of Education in Texas* (New York: Macmillan Company, 1925); and C. E. Evans, *The Story of Texas Schools* (Austin: Steck Company, 1955). Both of these volumes deal with the Tejano experience in Texas education in only a cursory manner. Among the volumes and articles that do address the experience of Mexican Americans in education are Meyer Weinberg, *A Chance to Learn: A History of Race and Education in the United States* (Cambridge, Eng.: Cambridge University Press, 1977); Guadalupe San Miguel, Jr., "Mexican American Organizations and the Chang-

ing Politics of School Desegregation in Texas, 1945–1980," *Social
Science Quarterly* 63 (December 1982) 701–15; Guadalupe San
Miguel, Jr., "The Struggle against Separate and Unequal Schools:
Middle Class Mexican Americans in the Desegregation Campaign
in Texas, 1929–1957," *History of Education Quarterly* 23 (Fall
1983), 343–59; Guadalupe San Miguel, Jr., *"Let All of Them Take
Heed": Mexican Americans and the Campaign for Educational
Equality in Texas, 1910–1981* (Austin: University of Texas Press,
1987); and Guadalupe San Miguel, Jr., "Endless Pursuits: Mexican
American Educational Experience in Corpus Christi, Texas, 1880–
1960" (Ph.D. diss., Stanford University, 1979).

3. This is not to be construed as a disparaging remark. While
the question of cause-and-effect relations between formal education and modernization is not of great import for an analysis
of the Tejanos' experience with the evolving Texas school system in the nineteenth century, it is of crucial significance for any
complete understanding of modernization and its problems in the
contemporary world. For an excellent analysis of policy issues and
connections between education and modernization (especially the
economic aspects of modernization) see Lascelles Anderson and
Douglas M. Windham, eds., *Education and Development: Issues
in the Analysis and Planning of Postcolonial Societies* (Lexington,
Mass.: Lexington Books, 1982).

4. The nation-building function is central to Val D. Rust's
analysis of the development of formal school systems in the modern era, and the work-force aspects are integral to the collection
of articles assembled by Anderson and Windham on contemporary
issues and connections between education and global modernization. See Rust, *Alternatives in Education,* and Anderson and
Windham, *Education and Development.* In an excellent and pro-
vocative analysis of the evolution of education in the United States,
Joel Spring argues that these two instrumental uses, and especially the work-force development function, have served as anchor
points for the establishment of national educational policy since
the end of World War II. See Joel Spring, *The Sorting Machine:
National Educational Policy Since 1945* (New York: David McKay
Company, 1976). These same two functional connections between
schooling and modernization are also fundamental to the scholarly
concerns of many works dealing with the educational status and
needs of minorities. For example Herschel T. Manuel's monograph,
*Spanish-Speaking Children of the Southwest: Their Education and
the Public Welfare* (Austin: University of Texas Press, 1965) con-

this century. The nineteenth-century data are of such quality that to attempt the construction of a social-class scale would result in numerous misclassifications, leading to the historiographic error of presentism. What may appear to be "lower" socioeconomic standing through the lenses of twentieth-century statistical models may not have been "lower" standing in communities of the nineteenth century. While we agree that social class probably intersected ethnicity in affecting inequalities of education, such influences are best dealt with on the basis of ethnographic information such as that in Montejano's and San Miguel's works. This aside, the data from the nineteenth century clarify the presence of aggregate inequalities of education based on ethnicity.

23. In the closing decades of the nineteenth century, the Census Bureau began measuring literacy by degrees as well as by its simple presence or absence in the population. For example persons who could read but not write, or write but not read, were indicated as having achieved a degree of literacy without being counted as fully literate. In this discussion of literacy, those who had achieved any degree of literacy are included as literates for the purpose of calculations and estimates.

24. These estimates are derived from information reported in *U.S. Census of Population,* 1850.1, tables XLIII and XXI–XXIL, pp. lxi and xlii–xliii; and 1900.2, tables LVII, LVIII, LIX, LXVII, and LXVIII, pp. ciii, civ, cv, cxv, and cxvi. A central reason for the lack of increase in the statewide rate of literacy is that blacks, then recently freed from slavery, were included in the literacy calculations for the decades after the Civil War.

25. These estimates were derived by taking the number of illiterate Tejanos estimated from our data over the number of illiterates in the state as estimated from *U.S. Census of Population,* 1850.1, tables XLIII and XXI–XXII, pp. lxi and xlii–xliii; and 1900.2, tables LVII, LVIII, LIX, LXVII, and LXVIII, pp. ciii, civ, cv, cxv, and cxvi.

26. The literacy rates of Tejanos in the Mexican settlement region also were far below those of Anglos in the region. The Anglo rates were 93.4 percent in 1850 and 95.4 percent in 1900. Anglos simply were not disadvantaged as the Mexicans were by the delayed arrival of schools in the region.

27. Tejano immigrants and females particularly were affected by the obstacles to schooling in south, central, and west Texas. By the turn of the century, 47.5 percent of native-born Mexican adults were literate compared to just 34.6 percent of the immigrants from

Mexico. In the same year, 47.2 percent of Tejano males had learned to read and write, compared to only 29.6 percent of the Tejanas.

28. The lack of census figures for west Texas in 1850 prevents a comparison for that section. However, the labor force illiteracy rates for west Texas between 1860 and 1900 show a pattern similar to that of the southern section, although the 25 percent illiteracy rate in the west at the turn of the century was well below the rate of 47 percent for the south.

29. A worthwhile analysis of nineteenth-century public philosophy and its effects on the education of Mexicans is found in Gilbert G. Gonzales, "Segregation of Mexican American Children in a Southern California City: The Legacy of Expansionism and the American Southwest," *Western Historical Quarterly* 16 (January 1985) 55–57.

30. As the occupational standing of Mexican Americans deteriorated, female involvement in gainful employments increased. Between 1850 and 1900, the number of working Tejanas multiplied by 43 times, and this growth was considerably greater than the increase among Mexican-American male workers. Yet despite the rapid increase of female workers, they never comprised more than 12 percent of the total Tejano work force.

31. See Elise Boulding, *The Underside of History: A View of Women through Time* (Boulder, Colo.: Westview Press, 1976).

32. Detailed descriptions of the roles of mutual-aid associations in various European immigrant communities can be found in Louis Wirth, *The Ghetto* (Chicago: University of Chicago Press, 1936); Nathan Glazer, *American Judaism* (Chicago: University of Chicago Press, 1957); and W. I. Thomas and Florian Znaniecki, *The Polish Peasant in Europe and America* (New York: Dover Press, 1958). Stanford Lyman, *Chinese Americans* (New York: Random House, 1974), has clarified the same phenomenon in the Chinese American community.

33. This is not meant to imply either that organized activity for mutual aid was nonexistent among Tejanos, or that females were completely uninvolved with such matters. On the contrary José Amaro Hernández, *Mutual Aid for Survival: The Case of the Mexican American* (Malabar, Fl.: Krieger Publishing Co., 1983), makes it clear that mutual aid is a tradition in the Mexican-American community that dates back to at least the sixteenth century, and that women always have been welcome participants. Nevertheless Julie Leininger Pycior, "*La Raza* Organizes: Mexican American Life in San Antonio, 1915–1930 as Reflected in *Mutualista* Ac-

tivities" (Ph.D. diss., University of Notre Dame, 1979), 76–81, describes Mexicanas as "ambivalent about their role" in mutual-aid organizations as late as the twentieth century. Here we are saying only that Mexican-American females were hampered by illiteracy in their ability to take the same energetic roles that women of other ethnic immigrant origins played. This notwithstanding, mutual aid was an important aspect of Tejano life in the nineteenth century, including the struggle for the improvement of educational conditions.

34. This, of course, is contrary to the stereotype of the indolent immigrant who fails to comprehend the value of education. Nevertheless between 1880 and 1900, the only period for which the census provides sufficient information to identify the children of *inmigrantes,* the school-attendance rate for Tejano scholastics with one or both parents born in Mexico increased from 21.4 percent to 27.6 percent. At the same time, the rate for children of native parentage (both parents born in Texas) declined from 34.9 percent to 31.6 percent. Since the children of immigrants comprised more than four-fifths of the Mexican-American scholastic population, the determination of growing numbers of inmigrantes to make sure their children were schooled must be deemed an important factor in the resurgence of Tejano enrollments.

35. See Hernández, *Mutual Aid for Survival,* 64–67, for a discussion of these and other mutual-aid societies that emerged in Texas between 1870 and 1900.

36. Ibid., 70–71, 94, discusses mutual-aid efforts to improve the educational opportunities of Mexican Americans.

Chapter 5

1. Important contributions to this line of thought and research can be found in Gordon W. Allport, *The Nature of Prejudice* (New York: Doubleday, 1958), 250–68, and Muzafer Sherif and Carolyn W. Sherif, *Groups in Harmony and Tension: An Integration of Studies on Intergroup Relations* (New York: Harper and Row, 1953). More recent discussions are found in Vincent N. Parillo, *Strangers to These Shores,* 2d ed. (New York: John Wiley and Sons, 1985), 68–69, 76–77; and Rodney Stark, *Sociology,* 2d ed. (Belmont, Cal.: Wadsworth, 1985), 282–91. Other important contributions are Marvin B. Scott and Stanford M. Lyman, "Accounts," *American Sociological Review* 33 (February 1968) 40–62; Philip Mason, *Patterns of Dominance* (New York: Oxford Univer-

sity Press, 1970); Eliot Aronson and Neal Osherow, "Cooperation, Prosocial Behavior, and Academic Performance: Experiments in the Desegregated Classroom," *Applied Social Psychology Annual* 1 (1980) 163–96; Stanley Lieberson, *A Piece of the Pie: Blacks and White Immigrants Since 1880* (Berkeley: University of California Press, 1980); and Orlando Patterson, *Slavery and Social Death: A Comparative Study* (Cambridge, Mass.: Harvard University Press, 1982). In the field of Texas history, James E. Crisp, "Race, Revolution, and the Texas Republic: Toward a Reinterpretation," in Robert A. Calvert, ed., *Texas: The Military Tradition* (College Station: Texas A & M University Press, forthcoming), has discussed the plausibility of the idea that racist attitudes and beliefs toward Texas Mexicans grew out of conflict and competition with Anglos, rather than serving as antecedents to the historical tension between the two groups.

2. See Maxine Baca Zinn, "Chicano Family Research," *Journal of Ethnic Studies* 7 (Fall 1979), 59–63. See also Michael V. Miller, "Variations in Mexican American Family Life: A Review Synthesis of Empirical Research," *Aztlán: International Journal of Chicano Studies and the Arts* 9 (Summer/Fall 1978), 210–11, 215–17; and the more recent Norma Williams, *The Mexican American Family: Tradition and Change* (Dix Hills, N.Y.; General Hall, 1990), 9–12.

3. Other studies supporting the view that various family types have developed among Mexican Americans over time are Alfredo Mirandé, "The Chicano Family: A Reanalysis of Conflicting Views," *Journal of Marriage and the Family* 39 (November 1977) 747–56; Alfredo Mirandé and Evangelina Enríquez, *La Chicana: The Mexican American Woman* (Chicago: University of Chicago Press, 1979), 107–17; and Alfredo Mirandé, *The Chicano Experience: An Alternative Perspective* (Notre Dame, Ind.: University of Notre Dame Press, 1985), 147–52. See also Miller, "Variations in Mexican American Family Life," 209, 231; Richard Griswold del Castillo, *La Familia: Chicano Families in the Urban Southwest, 1848 to the Present* (Notre Dame, Ind.: University of Notre Dame Press, 1984); De León and Stewart, *Tejanos and the Numbers Game;* and Robert R. Alvarez, Jr., *Familia: Migration and Adaptation in Baja and Alta California, 1800–1975* (Berkeley: University of California Press, 1987).

4. A nuclear family is defined in this study as a family composed of a head of household, a spouse, and his or her offspring below age eighteen. Of course a family was classified as single-person when only one person was present in a household. The

extended family, however, is a more complex category. The most common concept of an extended family is the one popularly associated with agrarian life, consisting of a three-generation residential arrangement in which a married couple lives with their offspring, the spouses of offspring, and dependent grandchildren. Another type is the so-called stem family, involving the coresidence of a married offspring with his or her spouse, parents, and dependent children. A third type of extended arrangement is the joint family, in which two siblings, their spouses, and dependent children coreside. For each of these ideal types, moreover, permutations exist in reality; our classification of extended families sought to encompass all the variations. For a current discussion of basic family types see George E. Dickinson and Michael R. Leming, *Understanding Families: Diversity, Continuity, and Change* (Boston: Allyn and Bacon, 1990), 19–42.

5. Interestingly these data confirm Peter Laslett's counter to the idea that industrialization and modernization replaced the extended family with the nuclear family as the prevalent pattern. Instead, according to Laslett, the nuclear form was prevalent before the industrial revolution in England, as it was in our findings for both Tejanos and Anglos in Texas during the frontier era. See Peter Laslett, *The World We Have Lost: England before the Industrial Age*, 3d ed. (New York: Charles Scribner's Sons, 1984), 81–105.

6. See, for example, Leo Grebler, Joan W. Moore, and Ralph Guzmán, *The Mexican American People: The Nation's Second Largest Minority* (New York: Free Press, 1970), 352–54, 358; Griswold del Castillo, *La Familia,* 45, 47; Richard Griswold del Castillo, "'Only for my Family . . .': Historical Dimensions of Chicano Family Solidarity—The Case of San Antonio in 1860," *Aztlán: International Journal of Chicano Studies Research* 16 (1985) 165–71; and Thomas E. Sheridan, *Los Tucsonenses: The Mexican American Community in Tucson, 1854–1941* (Tucson: University of Arizona Press, 1986), 135, 137–38, 140.

7. De León and Stewart, *Tejanos and the Numbers Game,* 49–65.

8. The theme that industrialization, modernization, and urbanization have contributed to diverse and malleable family and household patterns among Anglos, Mexican Americans, blacks, and Americans of differing social classes is central to the comprehensive analysis of American families by Maxine Baca Zinn and D. Stanley Eitzen, *Diversity in Families,* 2d ed.(New York: Harper and Row, 1991).

9. These works include Raymund Paredes, "The Image of the

Mexican in American Literature" (Ph.D. diss., University of California, Berkeley, 1974); and Raymund Paredes, "The Mexican Image in American Travel Literature," *New Mexico Historical Review* 52 (January 1977) 5–29. See also see Crisp, "Anglo-Texan Attitudes"; Cecil Robinson, *Mexico and the Hispanic Southwest in American Literature* (Tucson: University of Arizona Press, 1977); and De León, *They Called Them Greasers.*

10. Elizabeth York Enstam, "The Family," in Robert F. O'Conner, ed., *Texas Myths* (College Station: Texas A & M University Press, 1986), 143.

11. De León, *They Called Them Greasers*, 15.

12. Gilbert D. Kingsbury, "Texas: The Río Grande Valley: Cortina" (typescript, Kingsbury Papers, Barker Texas History Center, University of Texas Archives, Austin), 146.

13. De León, *They Called Them Greasers*, 24.

14. For a complete discussion of these Anglo views see ibid., chapter 4, 36–48.

15. Ibid., 37.

16. This expressive form of commentary can be found in the travel accounts of Anglo men who visited Texas during the years of the republic. See, for example, Francis S. Latham, *Travels in Texas, 1842*, ed. by Gerald S. Pierce (Austin: Encino Press, 1971), 37–38.

17. As quoted in De León, *They Called Them Greasers*, 39, from Andrew Forest Muir, ed., *Texas in 1837: An Anonymous Contemporary Narrative* (Austin: University of Texas Press, 1958), 103.

18. As quoted in ibid., 43, from Frederick Law Olmsted, *A Journey Through Texas: Or a Saddle-Trip on the Southwestern Frontier; with a Statistical Appendix* (New York: Dix, Edwards and Co., 1857; reprint Austin: University of Texas Press, 1978), 151–52, 161.

19. As quoted in ibid., 46, from *San Angelo Standard*, 21 September 1889, p. 1.

20. Crisp, "Race, Revolution, and the Texas Republic."

21. David J. Weber, "Commentary," unpublished comments concerning James Crisp's, "Race, Revolution, and the Texas Republic," presented at the annual meeting of the Texas State Historical Association, Austin, Texas, 1986.

22. Crisp, "Race, Revolution, and the Texas Republic."

23. Ibid. See also George M. Frederickson, "Toward a Social Interpretation of the Development of American Racism," in Nathan I. Huggins, Martin Kilson, and Daniel M. Fox, eds.,

Key Issues in the Afro-American Experience vol. 1 (San Diego: Harcourt, Brace, Jovanovich, 1971), 240–54.

NOTES TO
PAGES 84–90

24. Crisp, "Race, Revolution, and the Texas Republic."

25. Weber, "Commentary." See also David J. Weber, *Myth and the History of the Hispanic Southwest* (Albuquerque: University of New Mexico Press, 1988), 143 n. 33.

26. Enstam, "The Family," 148.

27. Ibid., 153–54.

28. See De León, *They Called Them Greasers,* chapters 3 and 5.

29. *El Paso Herald,* 8 July 1897, p. 2.

30. De León, *The Called Them Greasers,* 49.

31. The phrase is from the title of David J. Weber, *Foreigners in Their Native Land: Historical Roots of the Mexican Americans* (Albuquerque: University of New Mexico Press, 1973).

32. The development of the Texas economy between 1900 and 1930 is discussed in Robert A. Calvert and Arnoldo De León, *The History of Texas* (Arlington Heights, Ill.: Harlan Davidson, 1990), chapter 9.

33. Arthur Corwin, *Immigrants—and Immigrants: Perspectives on Mexican Labor Migration to the United States* (Westport, Conn.: Greenwood Press, 1978), 110, 116.

34. For a discussion of procedures employed by Anglos in securing cheap Mexican labor during this period, see Montejano, *Anglos and Mexicans.*

35. Mario T. García, "Americanization and the Mexican Immigrant, 1880–1930," *Journal of Ethnic Studies* 6 (Summer 1978) 19.

36. See García, ibid., 21–25.

37. Carole E. Christian, "Joining the American Mainstream: Texas's Mexican Americans During World War I," *Southwestern Historical Quarterly* 92 (April 1989) 559–95.

38. Guadalupe San Miguel, Jr., *"Let All of Them Take Heed,"* 25, 19.

39. As quoted in García, "Americanization and the Mexican Immigrant," 30–31, from *Reports of the Public Schools* (El Paso, 1903–04), 26. For an extended discussion of the drive toward Americanization of Mexican-American students in Texas during the 1920s, see San Miguel, *"Let All of Them Take Heed,"* chapter 2.

Epilogue

1. Alfredo Mirandé argues that the phenomenon of conquest as an element shaping the values and orientations of Chicano culture not only stems from the American takeover of the Southwest, but from the Spanish conquest of Mexico dating further back in time. See Mirandé, *The Chicano Experience,* chapter 6.

2. Examples of recent studies that see Mexican-American history as that of a people entering the United States from Mexico, undergoing acculturation, and pursuing improved living standards are Mario T. García, *Mexican Americans: Leadership, Ideology, and Identity, 1930–1960* (New Haven, Conn.: Yale University Press, 1989); De León, *Ethnicity in the Sunbelt;* and Richard A. García, *Rise of the Mexican American Middle Class: San Antonio, 1929–1941* (College Station: Texas A & M University Press, 1991).

3. For an extensive discussion of the treaty that transferred the Hispanic Southwest to the United States, see Richard Griswold del Castillo, *The Treaty of Guadalupe Hidalgo: A Legacy of Conflict* (Norman: University of Oklahoma Press, 1990).

4. Weber, *Foreigners in Their Native Land.*

5. For examples of studies focusing on the contemporary Mexican-American community that accept its diversity, see Susan E. Keefe and Amado M. Padilla, *Chicano Ethnicity* (Albuquerque: University of New Mexico Press, 1987); and David L. Torres, "Dynamics behind the Formation of a Business Class: Tucson's Hispanic Business Elite," *Hispanic Journal of Behavioral Sciences* 22 (February 1990) 25–49. Beyond the growing recognition of diversity within the contemporary community, however, our contention is that the Mexican American, or at least the Tejano, community originated as a diverse and diversifying one. It has not evolved from homogeneity to diversity in the twentieth century; it embodies a tradition and heritage of change, adaptation, and diversification.

6. Such an approach is taken in Rupert Richardson et al., *Texas: The Lone Star State,* 5th ed. (Englewood Cliffs, N.J.: Prentice-Hall, 1988); and Seymour V. Connor, *Texas: A History* (Arlington Heights, Ill.: Harlan Davidson, 1971). See also Stephen Stagner, "Epics, Sciences, and the Lost Frontier: Texas Historical Writings, 1836–1936," *Western Historical Quarterly* 12 (April 1981) 165–81.

7. This recognition is also present in Calvert and De León, *The History of Texas.*

Bibliography

Primary Sources

Archival Records

Kingsbury, Gilbert D. "Texas: The Río Grande Valley: Cortina." (typescript, Kingsbury Papers, Barker Texas History Center, University of Texas Archives, Austin).

Books

Daniell, L. E. *Types of Successful Men of Texas*. Austin: publ. by the author; Eugene Von Boeckman, Printer and Bookbinder, 1890.

Latham, Francis S. *Travels in Texas, 1842*. Ed. by Gerald S. Pierce. Austin: Encino Press, 1971.

Muir, Andrew Forest, ed. *Texas in 1837: An Anonymous Contemporary Narrative*. Austin: University of Texas Press, 1958.

Olmsted, Frederick Law. *A Journey through Texas: Or a Saddle-Trip on the Southwestern Frontier. With a Statistical Appendix*. New York: Dix, Edwards and Co., 1857; reprint Austin: University of Texas Press, 1978.

Sutherland, Mary A. *The Story of Corpus Christi*, ed. by Frank B. Harrison. Houston: Rein and Sons, 1916.

Articles

Almonte, Juan N. "Statistical Report on Texas." Trans. by Carlos E. Castañeda. *Southwestern Historical Quarterly* 28 (January 1925) 177–222.

BIBLIOGRAPHY   *Census Materials*

Historical Statistics of the United States: Colonial Times to 1970.
     2 parts. Washington, D.C.: U.S. Bureau of the Census, 1975.
Population Schedules of the Census of the United States. 1850,
     1860, 1870, 1880, 1900.
United States Census of Population, ser. nos. 1850.1–1900.22,
     microfilmed from the holdings of the Social and Economic
     Statistics Administration Library (formerly the Bureau of the
     Census Library), Suitland, Md. (New Haven: Research Publi-
     cations, Inc.).

Government Documents

*Report of the Industrial Commission on Agriculture and Taxation
     in Various States,* vol. 11. Washington, D.C.: U.S. Government
     Printing Office, 1901.
*A Report of the Results of the Texas Statewide School Adequacy
     Survey.* Austin: Texas State Board of Education, 1937.
Reports of the Public Schools. El Paso, 1903–04.
Texas Legislature. *Members of the Texas Legislature, 1846–1962.*
     Austin: Fifty-Seventh Legislature, 1962.

Newspapers

Corpus Christi *Weekly Caller.* Corpus Christi, Texas, 1885.
Dallas *Weekly Herald.* Dallas, Texas, 1877, 1878.
El Paso *Herald.* El Paso, Texas, 1897.
San Angelo *Standard.* San Angelo, Texas, 1889.
San Angelo *Standard-Times.* San Angelo, Texas, 1937.
San Antonio *Express,* San Antonio, Texas, 1877, 1879, 1897, 1898.

Secondary Sources

Books

Achor, Shirley. *Mexican Americans in a Dallas Barrio.* Tucson:
     University of Arizona Press, 1978.
Acuña, Rodolfo. *Occupied America: The Chicano Struggle for
     Liberation.* San Francisco: Canfield Press, 1972.
———. *Occupied America: A History of Chicanos.* 3d ed. New
     York: Harper and Row, 1988.

Allport, Gordon W. *The Nature of Prejudice*. New York: Doubleday, 1958.

Allswang, John M. *Bosses, Machines, and Urban Voters: An American Symbiosis*. Port Washington, N.Y.: Kennikat Press, 1977.

Alvarez, Robert R. *Familia: Migration and Adaptation in Baja and Alta California, 1800–1975*. Berkeley: University of California Press, 1987.

Anders, Evan. *Boss Rule in South Texas: The Progressive Era*. Austin: University of Texas Press, 1982.

Anderson, Lascelles, and Douglas E. Windham, eds. *Education and Development: Issues in the Analysis and Planning of Postcolonial Societies*. Lexington, Mass.: Lexington Books, 1982.

Barr, Alwyn. *Reconstruction to Reform: Texas Politics, 1876–1906*. Austin: University of Texas Press, 1971.

Barrera, Mario. *Race and Class in the Southwest: A Theory of Racial Inequality*. Notre Dame, Ind.: University of Notre Dame Press, 1979.

Berger, Peter L., Brigette Berger and Hansfried Kellner. *The Homeless Mind: Modernization and Consciousness*. New York: Vintage Books, 1973.

Boulding, Elise. *The Underside of History: A View of Women through Time*. Boulder, Colo.: Westview Press, 1976.

Buenger, Walter L. *Secession and the Union in Texas*. Austin; University of Texas Press, 1984.

Calvert, Robert A., and Arnoldo De León. *The History of Texas*. Arlington Heights, Ill.: Harlan Davidson, 1990.

Campbell, Randolph B. *An Empire for Slavery: The Peculiar Institution in Texas*. Baton Rouge: Louisiana State University Press, 1989.

Castañeda, Carlos Eduardo. *The Mission Era: The Winning of Texas, 1693–1751*. Vol. 2 of Carlos Eduardo Castañeda, *Our Catholic Heritage in Texas, 1519–1936*. 7 vols. Austin: Boeckmann-Jones Company, 1936; reprinted, New York: Arno Press, 1976.

Church, Robert L. *Education in the United States: An Interpretive History*. New York: Free Press, 1976.

Connor, Seymour V. *Texas: A History*. Arlington Heights, Ill.: Harlan Davidson, 1971.

Corwin, Arthur. *Immigrants—and Immigrants: Perspectives on Mexican Labor Migration to the United States*. Westport, Conn.: Greenwood Press, 1978.

Dawson, Joseph Martin. *José Antonio Navarro: Co-Creator of Texas*. Waco, Tex.: Baylor University Press, 1969.

De León, Arnoldo. *Ethnicity in the Sunbelt: A History of Mexican Americans in Houston*. Houston: Mexican American Studies Program, University of Houston, 1989.

——— (with a contribution by Kenneth L. Stewart). *The Tejano Community, 1836–1900*. Albuquerque: University of New Mexico Press, 1982.

———. *They Called Them Greasers: Anglo Attitudes toward Mexicans in Texas*. Austin: University of Texas Press, 1983.

De León, Arnoldo, and Kenneth L. Stewart. *Tejanos and the Numbers Game: A Socio-Historical Interpretation from the Federal Censuses, 1850–1900*. Albuquerque: University of New Mexico Press, 1989.

Dickinson, George E., and Michael R. Leming. *Understanding Families: Diversity, Continuity, and Change*. Boston: Allyn and Bacon, 1990.

Eby, Frederick. *The Development of Education in Texas*. New York: Macmillan Company, 1925.

Evans, C. E. *The Story of Texas Schools*. Austin: Steck Company, 1955.

Foley, Douglas E., Clarice Mota, Donald E. Post, and Ignacio Lozano. *From Peones to Politicos: Ethnic Relations in a South Texas Town, 1900–1977*. 2nd ed. Austin: Center for Mexican American Studies, University of Texas, 1988.

García, Mario T. *Desert Immigrants: The Mexicans of El Paso, 1880–1920*. New Haven, Conn.: Yale University Press, 1981.

———. *Mexican Americans: Leadership, Ideology, and Identity, 1930–1960*. New Haven, Conn.: Yale University Press, 1989.

García, Richard A. *Rise of the Mexican American Middle Class: San Antonio, 1929–1941*. College Station: Texas A & M University Press, 1991.

Glazer, Nathan. *American Judaism*. Chicago: University of Chicago Press, 1957.

Grebler, Leo, Joan W. Moore, and Ralph Guzmán. *The Mexican American People: The Nation's Second Largest Minority*. New York: Free Press, 1970.

Grimm, Agnes G. *Llanos Mesteñas: Mustang Plains*. Waco, Tex.: Texian Press, 1968.

Griswold del Castillo, Richard. *La Familia: Chicano Families in the Urban Southwest, 1848 to the Present*. Notre Dame, Ind.: University of Notre Dame Press, 1984.

————. *The Treaty of Guadalupe Hidalgo: A Legacy of Conflict.* Norman: University of Oklahoma Press, 1990.

Hernández, José Amaro. *Mutual Aid for Survival: The Case of the Mexican American.* Malabar, Fl.: Krieger Publishing Co., 1983.

Hinojosa, Gilberto M. *A Borderlands Town in Transition: Laredo, 1755–1870.* College Station: Texas A & M University Press, 1983.

Jackson, Jack. *Los Mesteños: Spanish Ranching in Texas, 1721–1821.* College Station: Texas A & M University Press, 1986.

Jordan, Terry G. *Immigrants to Texas.* Boston: American Press, 1981.

————. *Trails to Texas: Southern Roots of Western Ranching.* Lincoln: University of Nebraska Press, 1981.

Katz, Michael B. *Class, Bureaucracy and Schools.* Expanded ed. New York: Praeger, 1975.

————. *The Irony of Early School Reform: Educational Innovation in Mid-Nineteenth Century Massachusetts.* Boston: Beacon Press, 1968.

Keefe, Susan E., and Amado M. Padilla. *Chicano Ethnicity.* Albuquerque: University of New Mexico Press, 1987.

Laslett, Peter. *The World We Have Lost: England before the Industrial Age.* 3d ed. New York: Charles Scribner's Sons, 1984.

Lathrop, Barnes F. *Migration into East Texas, 1835–1860.* Austin: Texas State Historical Association, 1949.

Lieberson, Stanley. *A Piece of the Pie: Blacks and White Immigrants since 1880.* Berkeley: University of California Press, 1980.

Long, Clarence D. *Wages and Earnings in the United States, 1860–1890.* New York: National Bureau of Economic Research, 1960.

Lyman, Stanford. *Chinese Americans.* New York: Random House, 1974.

Manuel, Herschel T. *Spanish-Speaking Children of the Southwest: Their Education and the Public Welfare.* Austin: University of Texas Press, 1965.

Mason, Philip. *Patterns of Dominance.* New York: Oxford University Press, 1970.

Meinig, D. W. *Imperial Texas: An Interpretive Essay in Cultural Geography.* Austin: University of Texas Press, 1969.

Mendelbaum, Seymour. *Boss Tweed's New York.* New York: John Wiley and Sons, 1965.

BIBLIOGRAPHY   Merton, Robert K. *Social Theory and Social Structure*. Glencoe,
Ill.: Free Press, 1957.

Miller, Zane. *Boss Cox's Cincinnati: Urban Politics in the Progressive Era*. New York: Oxford University Press, 1968.

Mirandé, Alfredo. *The Chicano Experience: An Alternative Perspective*. Notre Dame, Ind.: University of Notre Dame Press, 1985.

Mirandé, Alfredo, and Evangelina Enríquez. *La Chicana: The Mexican American Woman*. Chicago: University of Chicago Press, 1979.

Montejano, David. *Anglos and Mexicans in the Making of Texas, 1836–1986*. Austin: University of Texas Press, 1987.

Morton, Ohland. *Terán and Texas: A Chapter in Texas-Mexican Relations*. Austin: Texas State Historical Association, 1948.

Murguía, Edward. *Assimilation, Colonialism, and the Mexican American People*. Monograph 1. Austin: Center for Mexican American Studies and the University of Texas Press, 1975.

Paredes, Américo. *A Texas-Mexican Cancionero: Folksongs of the Lower Border*. Urbana: University of Illinois Press, 1976.

Parillo, Vincent N. *Strangers to These Shores*. 2d ed. New York: John Wiley and Sons, 1985.

Parry, J. H. *The Spanish Seaborne Empire*. New York: Alfred A. Knopf, 1966.

Patterson, Orlando. *Slavery and Social Death: A Comparative Study*. Cambridge, Mass.: Harvard University Press, 1982.

Poyo, Gerald E., and Gilberto M. Hinojosa. *Tejano Origins in Eighteenth-Century San Antonio*. Austin: University of Texas Press, 1991.

Reps, John W. *Cities of the American West: A History of Frontier Urban Planning*. Princeton, N.J.: Princeton University Press, 1979.

Richardson, Rupert N., Ernest Wallace, and Adrian Anderson. *Texas: The Lone Star State*. 5th ed. Englewood Cliffs, N.J.: Prentice-Hall, 1988.

Robinson, Cecil. *Mexico and the Hispanic Southwest in American Literature*. [Revision of *With the Ears of Strangers: The Mexican American in American Literature*]. Tucson: University of Arizona Press, 1977.

Rosenbaum, Robert. *Mexicano Resistance in the Southwest: "The Sacred Right of Self-Preservation."* Austin: University of Texas Press, 1981.

Rust, Val D. *Alternatives in Education: Theoretical and Historical*

Perspectives. Sage Studies in Social and Educational Change,
vol. 6. Beverly Hills, Cal.: Sage Publications, 1977.

Ryan, William. *Blaming the Victim.* New York: Pantheon Books, 1971.

Saldívar, Gabriel. *Documentos de la rebelión de Catarino E. Garza en la frontera de Tamaulipas y sur de Texas, 1891–1892.* Mexico City: Secretaría de Agricultura y Fomento, 1943.

Salinas, Martín. *Indians of the Río Grande Delta: Their Role in the History of Southern Texas and Northeastern Mexico.* Austin: University of Texas Press, 1990.

San Miguel, Jr., Guadalupe. *"Let All of Them Take Heed": Mexican Americans and the Campaign for Educational Equality in Texas, 1910–1981.* Austin: University of Texas Press, 1987.

Shannon, Fred A. *The Farmer's Last Frontier: Agriculture, 1860–1897. The Economic History of the United States,* vol 5. New York: Holt, Rinehart, and Winston, 1945.

Shelton, Edgar Greer. *Political Conditions among Texas Mexicans along the Río Grande.* San Francisco: R and E Research Associates, 1974.

Sheridan, Thomas E. *Los Tucsonenses: The Mexican American Community in Tucson, 1854–1941.* Tucson: University of Arizona Press, 1986.

Sherif, Muzafer, and Carolyn W. Sherif. *Groups in Harmony and Tension: An Integration of Studies on Intergroup Relations.* New York: Harper and Row, 1953.

Simmons, Ozzie G. *Anglo-Americans and Mexican Americans in South Texas.* New York: Arno Press, 1974.

Spratt, John S. *The Road to Spindletop: Economic Change in Texas, 1875–1901.* Dallas: Southern Methodist University Press, 1955.

Spring, Joel. *The Sorting Machine: National Educational Policy since 1945.* New York: David McKay Company, 1976.

Stark, Rodney. *Sociology.* 2d ed. Belmont, Cal.: Wadsworth, 1985.

Tarr, Joel A. *A Study of Boss Politics: William Lorimer of Chicago.* Chicago: University of Illinois Press, 1971.

Taylor, Paul S. *An American Mexican Frontier: Nueces County Texas.* Chapel Hill: University of North Carolina Press, 1934.

Thomas, W.I., and Florian Znaniecki. *The Polish Peasant in Europe and America.* New York: Dover Press, 1958.

Thompson, Jerry Don. *Vaqueros in Blue and Gray.* Austin: Presidial Press, 1976.

BIBLIOGRAPHY

Timmons, W. H. *El Paso: A Borderlands History*. El Paso: University of Texas at El Paso Press, 1990.

Toqueville, Alexis de. *Democracy in America*. Ed. by J. P. Mayer, trans. by George Lawrence. Garden City, N.Y.: Doubleday and Company, 1969.

Weber, David J. *Foreigners in Their Native Land: Historical Roots of the Mexican Americans*. Albuquerque: University of New Mexico Press, 1973.

———. *The Mexican Frontier, 1821–1846: The American Southwest under Mexico*. Albuquerque: University of New Mexico Press, 1982.

———. *Myth and the History of the Hispanic Southwest*. Albuquerque: University of New Mexico Press, 1988.

———, ed. *Troubles in Texas: A Tejano Viewpoint from San Antonio*. Dallas: DeGolyer Library at Southern Methodist University, 1983.

Weinberg, Meyer. *A Chance to Learn: A History of Race and Education in the United States*. Cambridge, Eng.: Cambridge University Press, 1977.

Wheeler, Kenneth W. *To Wear a City's Crown: The Beginnings of Urban Growth in Texas, 1836–1865*. Cambridge, Mass.: Harvard University Press, 1968.

Williams, Norma. *The Mexican American Family: Tradition and Change*. Dix Hills, N.Y.: General Hall, 1990.

Wirth, Louis. *The Ghetto*. Chicago: University of Chicago Press, 1936.

Zinn, Maxine Baca, and D. Stanley Eitzen. *Diversity in Families*. 2d ed. New York: Harper and Row, 1991.

Articles

Acuña, Rodolfo. "The Making of *Occupied America*." In Tatcho Mindiola, E., *Occupied America: A Chicano History Symposium*, 14–27. Monograph 3. Houston: Mexican American Studies Program, University of Houston, 1982.

Aronson, Eliot, and Neal Osherow. "Cooperation, Prosocial Behavior, and Academic Performance: Experiments in the Desegregated Classroom." *Applied Social Psychology Annual* 1 (1980) 163–96.

Christian, Carole E. "Joining the American Mainstream: Texas's Mexican Americans during World War I." *Southwestern Historical Quarterly* 92 (April 1989) 559–95.

Crisp, James E. "Race, Revolution, and the Texas Republic: Toward a Reinterpretation." In Robert A. Calvert, ed. *Texas: The Military Tradition.* College Station: Texas A & M University Press, forthcoming.

Cuellar, Alfredo. "Perspective on Politics." In Joan W. Moore with Alfredo Cuellar, *Mexican Americans,* chap. 8. Englewood Cliffs, N.Y.: Prentice–Hall, 1970.

Cuthbertson, Gilbert M. "Catarino Garza and the Garza War." *Texana* 12 (1974) 335–48.

Davies, Christopher S. "Life at the Edge: Urban and Industrial Evolution of Texas, Frontier Wilderness—Frontier Space, 1836–1986." *Southwestern Historical Quarterly* 89 (April 1986) 443–554.

de la Teja, Jesús F. "Forgotten Founders: The Military Settlers of Eighteenth-Century San Antonio de Béxar." In Gerald E. Poyo and Gilberto M. Hinojosa, *Tejano Origins in Eighteenth-Century San Antonio,* 27–48. Austin: University of Texas Press, 1991.

de la Teja, Jesús F. and John Wheat. "Béxar: Profile of a Tejano Community, 1820–1832." *Southwestern Historical Quarterly* 89 (July 1985) 7–34.

De León, Arnoldo. "The Tejano Experience in Six Texas Regions." *West Texas Historical Association Yearbook* 65 (1989) 36–49.

———. "Tejano History Scholarship: A Review of the Recent Literature." *West Texas Historical Association Yearbook* 61 (1985) 116–33.

———. "Texas Mexicans: Twentieth Century Interpretations." In Walter L. Buenger and Robert A. Calvert, eds, *Texas through Time: Evolving Interpretations,* 20–49. College Station: Texas A & M University Press, 1991.

De León, Arnoldo, and Kenneth L. Stewart. "Education is the Gateway: Comparative Patterns of School Attendance and Literacy between Anglos and Tejanos in Three Texas Regions, 1850–1900." *Aztlán: International Journal of Chicano Studies Research* 16 (1985) 177–95.

De León, Arnoldo, and Kenneth L. Stewart. "Education, Literacy, and Occupational Structure in West Texas, 1860–1900." *West Texas Historical Association Yearbook* 14 (1984) 127–43.

De León, Arnoldo, and Kenneth L. Stewart. "Literacy among Inmigrantes in Texas, 1850–1900." *Latin American Research Review* 20 (3) (1985) 180–87.

———. "Lost Dreams and Found Fortunes: Mexican and American Immigrants in South Texas." *The Western Historical Quarterly* 14 (July 1983) 291–310.

———. "Tejano Demographic Patterns and Socio-Economic Development." *Borderlands Journal* 7 (Fall 1985) 1–9.

———. "Work Force Participation Rates Among Mexican Immigrant Women." *Borderlands Journal* 9 (Spring 1986) 69–74.

Dugas, Vera Lea. "Texas Industry, 1860–1880." *Southwestern Historical Quarterly* 59 (October 1955) 151–83.

Enstam, Elizabeth York. "The Family." In Robert F. O'Connor, ed., *Texas Myths*, 139–58. College Station: Texas A & M University Press, 1986.

Foley, Neil F. "Chicanos and the Culture of Cotton in South Texas, 1880–1900: Reshaping Class Relations in the South." In Mary Romero and Cordelia Candelaria, eds, *Community Empowerment and Chicano Scholarship*, 111–26. Los Angeles: National Association for Chicano Studies, 1992.

Franklin, John Hope. "The Land of Room Enough." *Daedalus* 110 (Spring 1981) 1–12.

Frederickson, George M. "Toward a Social Interpretation of the Development of American Racism." In Nathan I. Huggins, Martin Kilson, and Daniel M. Fox, eds, *Key Issues in the Afro-American Experience,* vol. 1, 240–54. San Diego: Harcourt, Brace, Jovanovich, 1971.

García, Mario T. "Americanization and the Mexican Immigrant, 1880–1930." *Journal of Ethnic Studies* 6 (Summer 1978) 19–34.

González, Gilbert G. "Segregation of Mexican American Children in a Southern California City: The Legacy of Expansionism and the American Southwest." *The Western Historical Quarterly* 16 (January 1985) 55–76.

Griswold del Castillo, Richard. "'Only for my Family . . .': Historical Dimensions of Chicano Family Solidarity—The Case of San Antonio in 1860." *Aztlán: International Journal of Chicano Studies Research* 16 (1985) 165–71.

Guzmán, Ralph. "The Function of Anglo-American Racism in the Political Development of Chicanos." In F. Chris García, ed. *La Causa Politica: A Chicano Politics Reader,* 19–35. Notre Dame, Ind.: University of Notre Dame Press, 1974.

Hinojosa, Gilberto M., and Anne A. Fox. "Indians and Their Culture in San Fernando de Béxar." In Gerald E. Poyo and Gilberto M. Hinojosa, *Tejano Origins in Eighteenth-Century San Antonio,* 105–120. Austin: University of Texas Press, 1991.

Jordan, Terry G. "The Imprint of the Upper and Lower South on Mid-Nineteenth Century Texas." *Annals of the Association of American Geographers* 57 (1967) 667–90.

———. "Population Origins in Texas, 1850." *Geographical Review* 59 (January 1969) 83–103.

Miller, Michael V. "Variations in Mexican American Family Life: A Review Synthesis of Empirical Research." *Aztlán: International Journal of Chicano Studies and the Arts* 9 (Summer/Fall 1978) 209–31.

Mirandé, Alfredo. "The Chicano Family: A Reanalysis of Conflicting Views." *Journal of Marriage and the Family* 39 (November 1977) 747–56.

Paredes, Raymund. "The Mexican Image in American Travel Literature." *New Mexico Historical Review* 52 (January 1977) 5–29.

Poyo, Gerald E. "The Canary Islands Immigrants of San Antonio: From Ethnic Exclusivity to Community in Eighteenth-Century Béxar." In Gerald E. Poyo and Gilberto M. Hinojosa, *Tejano Origins in Eighteenth-Century San Antonio*, 49–58. Austin: University of Texas Press, 1991.

———. "Immigrants and Integration in Late Eighteenth-Century Béxar." In Gerald E. Poyo and Gilberto M. Hinojosa, *Tejano Origins in Eighteenth-Century San Antonio*, 85–103. Austin: University of Texas Press, 1991.

Rodríguez-O, Jaime E. "La Constitución de 1824 y la formación del Estado Mexicano." *Historia Mexicana* 40 (January/February, 1991) 507–35.

San Miguel, Jr., Guadalupe. "Mexican American Organizations and the Changing Politics of School Desegregation in Texas, 1945–1980." *Social Science Quarterly* 63 (December 1982) 701–15.

———. "Social and Educational Influences Shaping the Mexican American Mind." *Journal of Midwest History of Education Society* 14 (1986) 57–66.

———. "The Struggle against Separate and Unequal Schools: Middle Class Mexican Americans in the Desegregation Campaign in Texas, 1929–1957." *History of Education Quarterly* 23 (Fall 1983) 343–59.

Scott, Marvin B., and Stanford M. Lyman. "Accounts." *American Sociological Review* 33 (February 1968) 40–62.

Stagner, Stephen. "Epics, Sciences, and the Lost Frontier: Texas Historical Writings, 1836–1936." *Western Historical Quarterly* (April 1981) 165–81.

Thompson, Jerry Don. "The Many Faces of Juan Nepomuceno Cortina." *South Texas Studies,* vol. 2. Victoria, Texas: Victoria College Press, 1991: 85–98.

Timmons, W. H. "The Population of the El Paso Area—A Census of 1784." *New Mexico Historical Review* 52 (October 1977) 311–16.

Tjarks, Alicia V. "Comparative Demographic Analysis of Texas, 1777–1793." *Southwestern Historical Quarterly,* 77 (January 1974) 322–28.

Torres, David L. "Dynamics behind the Formation of a Business Class: Tucson's Hispanic Business Elite." *Hispanic Journal of Behavioral Sciences* 22 (February 1990) 25–49.

Tyler, Daniel, "The Mexican Teacher." *Red River Valley Historical Review* 1 (Autumn 1974) 207–10.

White, Richard. "Outlaw Gangs of the Middle Border: American Social Bandits." *Western Historical Quarterly* 12 (October 1981) 387–408.

Zinn, Maxine Baca. "Chicano Family Research." *Journal of Ethnic Studies* 7 (Fall 1979) 59–63.

Unpublished Papers, Theses, and Dissertations

Calderón, Roberto R. "The Mexican Electorate and Politics in South Texas, 1865–1881." (Paper presented at the XVI National Association for Chicano Studies Conference, Boulder, Colo., 14–16 April 1988).

Crisp, James Ernest. "Anglo-Texan Attitudes toward the Mexicans, 1821–1845" Ph.D. diss., Yale University, 1976.

Douglas, James Ridley, "Juan Cortina: El Caudillo de la Frontera," M.A. thesis, University of Texas at Austin, 1987.

Paredes, Raymund. "The Image of the Mexican in American Literature." Ph.D. diss., University of California at Berkeley, 1974.

Peters, Robert Kingsley. "Texas: Annexation to Secession." Ph.D. diss., University of Texas at Austin, 1977.

Pycior, Julie Leininger "*La Raza* Organizes: Mexican American Life in San Antonio, 1915–1930 as Reflected in *Mutualista* Activities." Ph.D. diss., University of Notre Dame, 1979.

Riley, John Denny. "Santos Benavides: His Influence on the Lower Río Grande, 1823–1891." Ph.D. diss., Texas Christian University, 1976.

San Miguel, Jr., Guadalupe. "Endless Pursuits: Mexican American Educational Experience in Corpus Christi, Texas, 1880–1960." Ph.D. diss., Stanford University, 1979.

142

Simmons, Thomas Edward. "The Citizen Factories: The Americanization of Mexican Students in Texas Public Schools, 1928–
1945." Ph.D. diss., Texas A & M University, 1976.

Weber, David J. "Commentary." (Comments concerning James E.
Crisp, "Race, Revolution, and the Texas Republic," presented
at the Annual Meeting of the Texas State Historical Association, Austin, Texas, 1986.

White, Michael Allen. "History of Education in Texas, 1860–
1884." Ed.D. diss., Baylor University, 1969.

Younker, Donna Lee. "Teacher Education in Texas, 1879–1919."
Ph.D. diss., University of Texas at Austin, 1964.

Zamora, Emilio. "Mexican Labor Activity in South Texas, 1900–
1920" Ph.D. diss., University of Texas at Austin, 1983.

Index

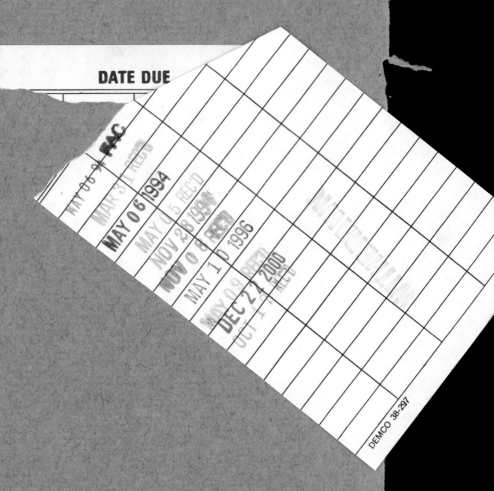